Strategy Central for the Active Reader

Literature

Lesli J. Favor, Ph.D.

AMSCO

Amsco School Publications, Inc.
315 Hudson Street, New York, N.Y. 10013

About the Author

Lesli J. Favor holds a Ph.D. in English from the University of North Texas. After graduating, she was assistant professor of English at Sul Ross State University Rio Grande College in southwest Texas. She left that position to be a full-time writer of books for school classrooms and libraries. In addition to this three-volume *Strategy Central* series, she is the author of eighteen other English/language arts and nonfiction texts. She lives near Seattle with her husband, young son, two dogs, and horse.

Consultant: John S. Mayher

John S. Mayher is professor of English education at New York University. Before going to NYU, he taught junior and senior high school in Massachusetts and California. A graduate of Harvard University, he is the author of *Uncommon Sense* and the coeditor of *Teaching English Today*.

Artist: David Pfendler

David Pfendler, a corn-fed Ohio native, started out as a pre-med student and fashion designer but gave it all up to pursue his dream of becoming an illustrator. He began by illustrating TV scripts for Levi's USA and now does international advertising campaigns as well as editorial and book projects. David's illustrations are created digitally, yet maintain a loose, hand-drawn feel. His clients include Abercrombie & Fitch, Levi's USA, Rolex, Axe, American Salon, and Vaseline. David lives and works in Greenwich Village, New York City.

Reviewers:

Joanna Exacoustos, UCLA Center X literacy coach and English teacher, Locke High School, Los Angeles, CA

Chantal Francois, doctoral student, Harvard Graduate School of Education, Cambridge, MA, and former humanities teacher, East Side Community High School, New York, NY

Leona Gross, humanities teacher, East Side Community High School, New York, NY

Cover Design: Wanda Kossak
Text Design & Composition: Nesbitt Graphics, Inc.
Line Art: Hadel Studio

Please visit our Web site at: *www.amscopub.com*

When ordering this book, please specify:
either **R 254 W** *or* STRATEGY CENTRAL FOR THE ACTIVE READER, LITERATURE

ISBN: 978-1-56765-172-0
NYC Item 56765-172-X

1 2 3 4 5 6 7 8 9 10   12 11 10 09 08

Contents

Introduction

When you hear the term "reading," you may think of a class you're in or a passage on a standardized test. But reading is something you do every day, and not just when you're in school. When you wake up, you may read a weather report online, or a five-day weather chart on TV. Then you may read the nutrition label on the side of a cereal box, or the puzzle on the back as you're pouring the flakes into your bowl. Then you read your textbook covers to make sure you take the right ones to school, and you read a text message from your friend asking to meet up by your locker. You read your class schedule, the manual that comes with your music player, and the application for the part-time job you'd like. When you get home, you read a note telling you to clean your room.

Reading is a crucial skill for all aspects of life. The ability to read and to think critically about what you've read will help you succeed in school, and also in the world around you—in the workplace, in your community, and even in your personal relationships.

The *Strategy Central* series is designed to give you the skills you need to read with more confidence. It contains strategies that active readers use to comprehend what they're reading. Every chapter contains two strategies, such as *finding word meaning in context* and *identifying conflict and resolution*. Under each strategy, you'll find the following sections.

Before You Read

This section is a warm-up that contains one or two fun activities to get you thinking about what you'll read and the strategy you'll use to read it.

While You Read

This section begins with a mini-lesson that explains the strategy in detail. In **Watch This,** you'll see how to think through the strategy, and in **Give It a Try,** you'll use it on your own as you read the **Reading Selection.** Finally, a **Read-Aloud Opportunity** offers you the chance to read the passage out loud, on your own or in groups, to help you further understand what you've read.

After You Read

Three sections—**Converse, Connect,** and **Write**—have you work independently and in small groups to talk, write about, and reflect on how you used the strategy and what you got out of the reading.

Think of *Strategy Central* as your toolbox. After you have worked with the strategies in each book, they will be your tools to use with anything you read—in school and out.

The **Literature** volume of *Strategy Central* brings you short stories, novel excerpts, and poems dealing with a variety of real issues, such as secrets between siblings, embarrassing moments in school, and guilt in a parent-child relationship. Literature is often described as both a window and a mirror . . . it helps you see other worlds, real and imaginary, and it is often also a reflection of the issues you face in your own life. Working through the Literature volume will help you get more from your reading, and it may even help you think about your life and the things that matter to you.

Consider your own reading habits and answer the following questions as best you can. There are no right or wrong answers; just write what comes to mind.

1 How or why do you consider yourself a reader?

2 What does it mean to be a "reader"?

3 What comes to mind when you see the word *literature*?

4 Book preferences (check as many as apply)

☐ If I'm reading a story with a first-person narrator (the person who tells the story refers to herself or himself as "I"), it matters to me if the narrator seems real or not.

☐ It matters if the narrator seems like someone I could be friends with.

☐ I care if the book I'm reading is based on a true story.

☐ I care if the book has themes or ideas I can relate to.

☐ I read fantasy.

☐ I read sci-fi.

☐ I read action-adventure.

☐ I read romance novels.

☐ I read young adult fiction.

☐ I read comedy.

☐ I read poetry.

☐ I read drama (plays).

☐ I usually read the same kinds of books.

☐ I like reading a lot of different kinds of books.

5 How do you choose literature to read? (check as many as apply)

☐ I read things that my friends recommend.

☐ I ask for recommendations from teachers or librarians.

☐ I browse the library/bookstores myself and find things that look interesting.

☐ I do searches on Web sites like amazon.com.

- ☐ I read only things my teacher makes us read.
- ☐ My parents give me books.
- ☐ I look at the front and back flaps.
- ☐ I read the first four pages.
- ☐ I look at the cover.
- ☐ I look at how long it is.

6 How do you read literature? (check as many as apply)

- ☐ I usually get bored or distracted when I read; it takes me forever to get through a book.
- ☐ I usually read a whole book very quickly; I have trouble putting it down.
- ☐ I skip over sections I don't understand.
- ☐ If I don't understand something, I give up on the book.
- ☐ I look up every word I don't know.
- ☐ If I don't understand a word, I skip over it.
- ☐ If I don't know a word, I try to guess what it means.
- ☐ If I don't understand something, I usually blame the author for being confusing.
- ☐ If I don't understand something, I usually blame myself for not getting it.
- ☐ I reread sections that I do not understand.
- ☐ I skim a lot.
- ☐ I read every word on the page.
- ☐ I take notes in the margins or on sticky notes.
- ☐ I sometimes use strategies such as making predictions and questioning when I read.

Chapter 1

Secrets

Reasons to Read

How often do you think about *why* you're reading something? Maybe you read a textbook chapter because a teacher assigned it—"I'm reading because I have to." Maybe you grab a graphic novel from a library shelf—"I'm reading this because it looked good." Maybe a friend always has the latest issue of a certain magazine, and you borrow it—"I'm reading to see what she thinks is so interesting."

If you've ever picked up a book, newspaper, or magazine for one of these reasons, you're in good company. But once you've picked something up, how do you make sure that you get something out of it? How can you be sure that you'll even understand what you read? This chapter answers these questions by providing you with strategies, including **setting a purpose for reading** and **monitoring your understanding**. With these strategies, you can make your reading experience more rewarding.

Strategy▶
Set a Purpose for Reading

Before You Read

(Anticipation Guide)

Directions: Read each statement and decide whether you agree or disagree with it. If you agree, write YES on the line under Before Reading. If you disagree, write NO. At the end of this chapter, you will return to this page to complete the After Reading column.

Before Reading		After Reading
_____	1. Teens should not keep secrets from their parents.	_____
_____	2. It's never okay to tell someone else's secret.	_____
_____	3. You should not keep secrets from someone you care about.	_____
_____	4. Everyone has the right to his or her own secrets, no matter how young he or she is.	_____
_____	5. What someone does not know won't hurt him.	_____

(Preview the Story)

Directions: Look at the reading selection on pages 6–9. Then jot down your reactions to the parts of the text listed in this table. There are no right or wrong answers; just write what comes to mind.

Text Element	Your Thoughts or Expectations of the Story, Based on This Element
Book title	
First few paragraphs	
Words or parts of the text that stand out	

While You Read

Reading Strategy Mini-Lesson

Reading Strategy ▶ Set a Purpose for Reading

You wake up on a Saturday morning. The whole day stretches before you, waiting to be filled. What do you do? You could lie there, hoping something good happens. Or you could decide exactly what you want to happen that day. Then you could haul yourself out of bed and make it happen.

In which scenario are you more likely to get what you want out of the day?

The same is true for reading a text—any text, whether it is a story, a poem, an article, or an e-mail. The words lie before you, waiting to be read. What do you do? You could run your eyes through the sentences, hoping that something will happen—you're just not sure what. Or you could **set a purpose for reading** to make sure that you get something out of the text.

Setting a purpose for reading means that you set a personal goal for reading the text. Your goal will vary depending on what kind of text it is. Here's how you might set your purpose for reading.

Setting a Purpose for Reading *To make sure I get something from the text*	
1. Preview the text.	Preview the text, as you did in the preview activity on page 2. Just like a movie preview, a text preview gives you an idea of what the text is about and whets your appetite.
2. Identify the genre (type) of text.	Identify whether the text is fiction (made-up characters and events) or nonfiction (facts and information). Let the type of text guide you in setting a purpose for reading.
3. Decide what you hope to gain from reading the text.	You may want to find out more about a particular character, or you may wonder what will happen in a key scene. You may want to learn specific facts about a topic or learn a process or procedure. You may want to laugh or be kept at the edge of your seat. Your goal for reading may or may not be the same as that of another reader.

Watch This!

The Strategy in Action

In the following table, you'll find a reading selection in the left-hand column. In the right-hand column is an example of how your thoughts might unfold as you set a purpose for reading this text.

Reading Selection	Set a Purpose for Reading
The Deserted Mansion "It looks so creepy," whispered Kitra. "I'm afraid to go in." "No one has lived there for thirty years," said Rachel. "We'll be fine. I just want to check it out." "Okay, but be really quiet. Don't make any noise," whispered Kitra. "What are you afraid of?" grumbled Rachel. "You don't believe in ghosts, do you? Stop being such a baby." *Creeeak.* The girls opened the front door. "It's so dark and dusty," whispered Kitra. "No furniture at all. I wonder if there's anything upstairs." *Crash.* "What was that noise?" shrieked Kitra. "Is there someone here?" "Let's get out of here," said Rachel. "Fast!" "I think I hear footsteps!" squealed Kitra. "Run!"	**1. Preview the text.** Okay, first I should preview the text. The title makes me expect something haunted and scary. The first four paragraphs hint at the house possibly being spooked. The two main characters seem to be Kitra and Rachel. **2. Identify the genre (type) of text.** Next I should identify the type of text that this is. The first two paragraphs contain dialogue between two characters. Also ghosts are mentioned. This is probably fiction—a made-up story. **3. Decide what you hope to gain from reading the text.** Now I should set my purpose for reading. Since the passage is fiction, I expect to be entertained. The crash and footsteps tell me that something scary is going to happen. My purpose for reading this text is to find out who was making the noise (a ghost or a person?) and whether the girls escape. Scary!

Give It a Try

Set a Purpose for Reading

Directions: The following table will help you set a purpose for reading the excerpt from *The Rules of Survival* by Nancy Werlin on pages 6–9. Read each step on the left and write your responses on the right.

Setting a Purpose for Reading
The Rules of Survival

Instructions	Your Responses
1. Preview the text. Review the ideas you recorded in the preview activity on page 2. If necessary, glance again at the selection. Write one or two sentences stating what kinds of things you expect from this text.	
2. Identify the genre (type) of text. Jot down clues that will help you identify whether the text is fiction or nonfiction. Then write the genre of the text.	
3. Decide what you hope to gain from reading the text. Based on the information you gathered in steps 1 and 2, decide what, in particular, you hope to gain by reading this text. Write a sentence stating your purpose for reading the text. Then turn the page and read it with your purpose in mind.	

Reading Selection

from The Rules of Survival

by Nancy Werlin

Dear Emmy,

As I write this, you are nine years old, too young to be told the full and true story of our family's past, let alone be exposed to my philosophizing about what it all meant. I don't know how old you'll be when you do read this. Maybe you'll be seventeen, like I am now. Or maybe much older than that—in your twenties or even thirties.

I have decided to write it all down for you, and I will, but that decision doesn't keep me from having doubts. I wonder if maybe it would be better if you never read this. I wonder if you really need to know exactly what happened to us—me, you, Callie—at the hands of our mother. As I sit here writing, part of me hopes that you go along happily your whole life and never need or want to know the details. I believe that's what Aunt Bobbie hopes for, and Callie. I can understand that. For example, I have to admit that I don't want to know any details about what happened when our mother kidnapped you—so long as you've forgotten it, anyway. So long as you're not having screaming nightmares or something.

But if you are reading this letter, that means you are about to find out everything I know. It means I will have decided to tell you—decided twice. Once, by writing it all down now. And then again, by giving this to you to read sometime in the future.

I hope my memories of that time won't always be as clear as they are now. As I write, I only have to focus and I'm there again, in the past. I'm thirteen and fourteen and fifteen—or younger. It was terrible living through it the first time, but I think it's going to be almost as bad to live through it once more on paper. To try . . . not just to get it all down accurately, but to understand it. I need to make sense of it. I need to try to turn the experience into something valuable for you, and for myself—not just something to be pushed away and forgotten.

Emmy, the events we lived through taught me to be sure of nothing about other people. They taught me to expect danger around every corner. They taught me to understand that there are people in this world who mean you harm. And sometimes, they're people who say they love you.

Matthew

1. Murdoch

For me, the story begins with Murdoch McIlvane.

I first saw Murdoch when I was thirteen years old. Callie was eleven, and Emmy, you were only five. Back then, you talked hardly at all. We weren't even sure if you'd be able to start school when you were supposed to in the fall. Don't misunderstand—we knew you were smart. But school, well, you know how they are, wanting everybody to act alike.

That particular night in August, it was over a hundred degrees, and so humid that each breath felt like inhaling sweat. It was the fourth day of a heat wave in Boston, and over those days, our apartment on the third floor of the house in Southie had become like the inside of an oven. However, it was a date night for our mother—Saturday—so we'd been locked in.

"I want my kiddies safe," Nikki had said.

Not that the key mattered. Once Callie and I heard you snoring—a soft little sound that was almost like a sigh—we slipped out a window onto the back deck, climbed down the fire escape, and went one block over to the Cumberland Farms store. We wanted a breath of air-conditioning, and we were thinking also about Popsicles. Red ones. I had a couple dollars in my pocket from the last time I'd seen my father. He was always good for a little bit of money, and the fact that it was just about all he was good for didn't make me appreciate the cash less.

It wasn't really his fault, that he was so useless. My dad was afraid of our mother. He kept out of her way. On the few occasions they were in the same room together, he wouldn't even meet her eyes. I didn't blame him for it too much. I understood. She was unpredictable.

I remember that night so well.

"We have to bring a Popsicle back for Emmy," Callie said, her flip-flops slapping against the pavement. "We can put it in the freezer for tomorrow."

I grunted. I didn't think there was enough money for three Popsicles, but if Callie wanted to sacrifice her own for you, knowing you would drip half of it onto your shirt, that was her business. For me, it was hard enough knowing that we couldn't stay long at the store, or even out on the street, where there was sometimes a breeze from the ocean a few blocks away. If you woke up and found you were alone, you might be scared. I'd decided we'd risk being away fifteen minutes. I glanced at my watch; it was only just before eight thirty and the sun hadn't quite gone below the horizon.

Doubt suddenly pushed at me. If you woke—or if our mother returned unexpectedly—

"Don't worry. Emmy won't wake up," Callie said. When it came to you, little sister, we always knew what the other was thinking. "And we'll be right back."

"Okay," I said. But I made a mental note to get us back in ten minutes rather than fifteen. Just in case. And next time, I'd let Callie go to the store alone. She was old enough, really. I'd stay with you. Or bring you, maybe.

It was hard to figure out what would be the safest thing to do, for all three of us, all the time. But it was my job. As we pushed open the door to the Cumberland Farms and were greeted by a glorious blast of cool air, I was thinking that in a year—year and a half—I could maybe go out by myself at night and trust Callie with you. Even if I could only do that once in a while, it would really help. I could get over to the ocean at night, walk the causeway, hang out with some of the guys from school. Maybe I could even talk to this one girl I sort of liked. If our mother were out anyway, it would be okay to leave you girls alone, I thought. I'd still be careful that you weren't alone with her when she came home after her Saturday night outings. That wouldn't be hard, considering she rarely came home before two or three in the morning. If at all.

> **Remember the purpose you set for reading. Is your main expectation being met?**

Then I saw him. Murdoch. Okay, I saw him but I didn't really see him. That came a few minutes later. I just glanced around the store. There was a teenager at the cash register behind the front candy counter. A huge, barrel-shaped man stood in front of the counter with a little boy, smaller even than you were then. And Murdoch (of course I didn't know his name then) and his date (a woman I never saw again) were in line behind the man with the boy.

Callie and I headed straight for the ice cream freezer, and we'd just reached it when the yelling began. We whipped around.

It was the barrel-shaped man and the little kid. The man had grabbed the boy by the upper arms and yanked him into the air. He was screaming in his face while the kid's legs dangled: *"What did you just do?"*

The little kid was clutching a package of Reese's Pieces and he started keening, his voice a long, terrified wail, his small body rigid.

The big man—his father?—shook him hard, and kept doing it.

"I'll teach you to take things without permission! Spend my money without asking!"

And then the other man, the one I later knew was called Murdoch, was between the father and son. Murdoch snatched the little kid away from his father and put the kid down behind him. Then Murdoch swiveled back.

to be continued

Read-Aloud Opportunity ▶ Chain Reading

Directions: Your teacher will appoint a reading leader. To start the activity, this leader reads aloud the first sentence in the reading selection, beginning on page 6. As soon as he or she finishes the sentence, the next person in line reads the next sentence aloud, and so on around the room. When the last person has read, the reading leader reads next, beginning the chain again. If someone has trouble reading a word, the reading leader should help by reading that word aloud for the person.

After You Read

Converse

Directions: With your teacher's guidance, form groups of four to five students. Choose a group leader to read the following conversation starters aloud. Then, each person chooses one of the conversation starters and uses it to help express personal ideas about the reading selection. After each person speaks, other group members may respond by expressing ideas or questions about what that person said.

Conversation Starters to Discuss *The Rules of Survival*

1. The part of the passage that interests me most is _____ because _____.
2. I don't completely understand the part about _____.
3. I agree/disagree with Matthew's decision to _____ because _____.
4. I think Matthew kept secrets from _____ because _____.
5. What surprised me most was _____.
6. I want to keep reading this story to find out _____.

Connect

Directions: Imagine that you board a bus and take your seat. On the seat, you find a battered notebook. On the cover is written *The Rules of Survival*. You open the notebook and see pages of handwriting. You begin to read, and what you read is the selection on pages 6–9.

You know that you can drop the notebook into the lost and found box at the front of the bus. But before doing so, you decide to write a letter to Matthew and tuck it into the notebook.

On your own paper, write a brief letter to Matthew in which you

(1) offer advice about how to deal with the situation he is in

or

(2) tell him about a similar experience that you or a friend went through, and how you or the friend handled the experience

or

(3) tell him how the events he described in the notebook made you feel.

Alternative: If you wish, you can write this as a dialogue between you and Matthew rather than as a letter.

Write

Directions: Review the information you recorded in Setting a Purpose for Reading, on page 5. Then, on your own paper, write one or two brief paragraphs in which you

- explain your purpose for reading the selection and what made you set that particular purpose.

- tell whether the selection met or did not meet your expectation, and why.

- explain one or two reasons why you would want to continue reading *The Rules of Survival.*

Strategy ▶
Monitor Your Understanding

You've seen how setting a purpose for reading can help you get more from what you read. You can look at your purpose for reading as a goal. To achieve that goal, you must understand the text when you read it. This section shows you how to **monitor your understanding** of what you read, as you read it. As a result, you can pinpoint when your understanding breaks down and take steps to fix it. The result is a more meaningful and satisfying reading experience.

Before You Read

IMO Table

Directions: With your teacher's guidance, form groups of two or three people. Together, complete the following steps.

1. *Sort the clue words.* The clue words in the table on the next page are taken from the passage you are about to read. Each word or phrase is part of the Characters, Setting, Problem, or Outcome in the story. Using each word or phrase only once, write the words in the box where you think they best fit. The Unknown Words box is for words whose meaning you do not know.

2. *Form an opinion.* Based on how you sorted the clue words, decide what will likely happen in the story. Using as many of the words as possible, write your opinion on the lines provided.

3. *Ask questions.* The clue words and your prediction may have left you wondering about certain words or details. In the "To find out" box, jot down what you want to find out when you read the selection.

IMO Table
To predict what will happen next, in my opinion, in The Rules of Survival

Clue Words

Murdoch	hurt	invisible coiled pulse
fear	kid	barrel-shaped man
counter	step back	
hustled	eyes bulged	

Characters	Setting	Problem
Outcome	**Unknown Words**	**To find out . . .**

In my opinion, what will happen is that . . . _____

_____

_____

_____

_____

_____

_____

Word Association

Directions: Draw a line down the center of a sheet of paper to form two columns. Label one column *Fear* and the other column *Safety.* Starting with *Fear,* spend five minutes jotting down phrases, words, and ideas that you associate with fear. Then spend five minutes jotting down things that you associate with safety. Your teacher may ask you to share your ideas with the class.

While You Read

Reading Strategy Mini-Lesson

Reading Strategy ▶ Monitor Your Understanding

Watching a DVD is easy, right? You just press Play to see the story come alive. As characters march across the screen and events unfold, you follow along. You may ask yourself, "Who is *that* supposed to be?" and press Pause while you connect the dots in your mind. You may ask, "What just happened?" and press Rewind to watch the scene again. You may watch scenes in slow motion, press Fast-Forward to peek ahead, or press Pause while you share opinions with a friend.

Wouldn't it be great if reading were this easy?

The truth is, effective readers use many of the same techniques that movie watchers use. Effective readers get results because they use their mental remote controls to help themselves understand what they are reading.

It all hinges on **monitoring your understanding**—in other words, being aware, as you read, of whether you are understanding what you read. To do this, ask yourself questions, just as you would while watching a movie. "Why is she so sad?" "Who is that supposed to be?" "What just happened?" "How did he know that?"

You may be able to answer your question right away and then keep reading. Often, however, the answer won't be obvious because your understanding has broken down. Think of the remote-control functions as **fix-up strategies**. You can fix up your understanding by pausing to think, rereading a sentence or paragraph, reading slowly, reading ahead, or stopping to get outside help.

The table on the next page shows three steps to monitoring your understanding.

Monitoring My Understanding *To make sure I understand what I read*	
1. Ask yourself questions as you read.	Ask specific questions such as, "Who said that?" "Why does he have so much money?" "How much time just passed?" or "Where is this scene happening?"
2. Stop when your understanding breaks down.	Stop reading when you cannot answer your question or when you first feel confused by the text. Identify what doesn't make sense. Is it a word? A sequence of events? The reason for a character's action? A character's identity?
3. Use one or more fix-up strategies to repair your understanding.	
Pause.	Stop reading and scan the text for clues to answer your question. Think about what you have already read.
Reread.	Go back to the last point where your understanding was clear and begin reading again from there.
Read slowly.	Read the confusing part slowly and thoughtfully. Try looking at it from another angle, such as from one of the characters' viewpoints.
Read ahead.	Keep reading and watch for details that can help you make sense of what was confusing.
Get outside help.	Look up an unfamiliar word in a dictionary, ask a friend or teacher to help you figure out a confusing scene, or find out about a topic in an encyclopedia.

Watch This!

The Strategy in Action

In the following table, you'll find a reading selection in the left-hand column. In the right-hand column is an example of how your thoughts might unfold as you monitor your understanding of this text.

Reading Selection	**Monitor Your Understanding**
The Face at the Window	So, Kyle must be the main character. What's going on? He's hot and thirsty. Why doesn't he just get a drink? What's an orb? Is it the sky? I've gotta reread . . . Oh, he's looking at the sun, so the orb must be the sun. And here's the problem, he's lost.
Kyle's forehead dripped with sweat, and his throat clenched in thirst. Turning his face to the sun, he squinted. The bright orb was well past its highest point and sliding west now. The day would end soon, and he would be out here alone, lost.	
"Keep going," he urged himself. "The campsite could be around the next bend in the canyon."	He must have wandered off from his campsite. He doesn't seem scared, though. He's the kind of person who stays calm in a crisis.
Forcing his tired feet to carry him forward, Kyle stumbled across rocks the size of grapefruits. Back at camp, cool water and grilled hot dogs waited for him. His mouth watered and his stomach knotted in hunger. Suddenly his ankle turned on a loose rock, and pain yanked him back to reality. "Get a grip," he told himself.	One second, he's walking in the canyon, then suddenly he's back at camp. What's going on? I'll read on . . . okay, that bit about food at camp was in his head. He's still lost.
Limping around a huge boulder, he stopped short, his jaw dropping. Rising at least a hundred feet above the canyon floor was an apartment house carved into the cliff's side. Small windows marked room after room stacked atop one another. No stairs were visible outside, and no doors opened at ground level.	This paragraph starts off with two complicated sentences. I'll reread them slowly. Okay, I can totally picture this, but why is an apartment house out here in a canyon? How do you get into it? I'm definitely curious.
Kyle recognized what it was at once. An abandoned home site of the Ancient Ones, the Anasazi. Then he saw a flicker of movement in one of the windows. Was that a face staring out at him? Maybe this place wasn't abandoned after all. Despite the afternoon sun, Kyle shivered.	Who are the Anasazi? Nothing here tells me. I'll look it up . . . Okay, the Anasazi were Native Americans who lived in the southwestern United States around 1200 B.C. Now Kyle sees something move in the window. Maybe it's a camper, but maybe the place is haunted. I'll keep reading to find out.

Give It a Try

Monitor Your Understanding

Directions

1. *Read.* On your own, read the second excerpt from *The Rules of Survival* which starts below. When you have a question or need help figuring out the meaning of the text, write a note in the margin or on a sticky note.

2. *Regroup and fix up.* When you have finished reading the selection, regroup with the class. Share an example of where your understanding of the text broke down. Referring to the fix-up strategies in the table on page 14, suggest and demonstrate strategies to work out the text's meaning.

Reading Selection

from The Rules of Survival

by Nancy Werlin

continued from page 9

Emmy, I like to freeze the memory in my mind and just look at Murdoch. He was a medium kind of man. Medium height, medium build, hair shaved close to the skull. You wouldn't look twice—until you have looked twice.

He wasn't afraid. I noticed that right away about him. Here was this huge enraged man, facing him. But this other man, Murdoch, was calm. At the same time, there was this tension coiling off him.

Callie and I were behind Murdoch and to the left, so we had only a partial view of his face and expression. But we had a full-on view of the barrel-shaped man. And we had a good view of the little kid, who was so shocked that he stopped crying and just stared up at Murdoch's back with his mouth open.

Meanwhile, Murdoch said quietly but audibly, "If you want to hurt somebody, you can hurt me. Go on. Hit me. I won't hit back. You can do it until you're not angry anymore. I'll let you."

There was an endless, oh, five seconds. The father's eyes bulged. His fists were clenched. He drew one arm back. But Murdoch was still looking straight at him, and I knew—you could feel it vibrating in the air—that even though Murdoch had said he wouldn't hit him, he wanted to. He wanted to hurt him.

I liked him for that. No, Emmy, I loved him for that. Immediately.

"Hit me," Murdoch said. "Come on. Better me than the kid. Why not? You want to."

And then it was all over. The man blinked and took a step back. He said something, loudly, about having had a hard day and it doesn't hurt a kid to learn to keep his hands to himself. And Murdoch was nodding even though I guessed that he was thinking what I was about that man. But Murdoch turned away from the father as if he was no threat anymore. He knelt on the floor in front of the little kid.

You could smell the kid's fear floating on the stale, air-conditioned store air. He stole one little look behind Murdoch at the big man, and you could see him thinking, *I'll have to pay for this later.*

But Murdoch talked directly to the kid. "It's wrong for anybody ever to hurt you. No matter who does it, it's wrong. Can you remember that?"

The kid's eyes were now huge. He looked at his father again. Then back at Murdoch. Then he nodded.

"You'll remember that?" Murdoch insisted. "You don't have to do anything else. You just have to remember."

He waited.

The kid nodded. Solemnly.

"Good," said Murdoch.

The kid reached out one hand toward him. In it was the package of Reese's Pieces. Murdoch took it and said, "Thank you." He stood up in one smooth motion. He put the package on the counter. But his eyes didn't leave the little boy. The little boy kept looking back, too, while the big man finished paying for his stuff and then hustled the kid outside.

As the door slammed behind them, there was complete silence in the store. It was then I realized that Callie had grabbed my hand and was holding it.

"Oh, hello?" said the woman who was with Murdoch. "Hello, Murdoch? You should have thought about me. What if there was a big fight and I got hurt? What kind of a date do you think that would be? Huh? Murdoch? Are you listening to me? Murdoch!"

Murdoch, I thought. It was a name I had never heard before. A strange name.

It suited him.

Murdoch didn't reply. His eyes had narrowed into slits. He held up the pack of Reese's Pieces and said to the teenage clerk, "I'll take these. And the ice coffee." The woman sighed and shrugged. She moved a step closer to Murdoch, but without even looking at her, he took a step away.

One more moment from my memory of that night: On his way out the door, Murdoch turned. He tossed the Reese's Pieces underhand to me and Callie. He smiled at us as he did it, but the smile didn't reach his eyes. And he wasn't thinking about us at all, or really seeing us. I could tell. Not the way he'd seen that little boy.

He was still giving off that invisible coiled pulse of—whatever it was.

He was still angry.

Then he was gone.

Read-Aloud Opportunity ▶ Radio Reading

Directions: Work in groups of three or four students.

1. *Prepare to read aloud.* In your group, divide the reading selection on pages 16–18 into three or four equal chunks. Assign one chunk to each group member. Take a few minutes to practice reading your chunk of text silently or in a whisper. Then, on a sheet of paper, write one question to ask your group about your section of text. It is okay if you do not know the answer to your question.

2. *Read aloud.* The person who has the first chunk of text reads it aloud to the group. The others listen carefully, their books closed. The reader then poses his or her question to the group, listens to their ideas, and offers ideas in return. Now the person with the next section of text reads, and so on, until each group member has taken a turn. Your teacher may ask groups to share their questions and answers with the class.

After You Read

Converse

Directions

1. *Think.* Read the question prompts in the box below and think about the excerpt from *The Rules of Survival.* On your own paper, write three questions that you have about the text. Use the prompts to help form your questions.

Question Prompts

Why did . . .

I don't get the part about . . .

Do you think that . . .

I wonder why the author . . .

Why is this [insert detail] in here . . .

What does this [insert detail] have to do with this [insert detail] . . .

---

2. *Pair.* Pair up with another student. One of you reads his or her first question aloud. The other person answers the question, giving reasons or examples. It may help to skim or reread the text for clues and ideas. Then switch roles, with the second person reading a question. Continue in this way until all of the questions are answered.

3. *Share.* Regroup with the whole class to share your ideas with the larger group.

Connect

Directions: With your teacher's guidance, form groups of five people. Each person takes one of the connection prompts on the next page. Connect to the text by thinking about what you know about the character and about people in real life who are similar to the character. Each person should use the connection prompt to express his or her ideas to the group. Group members may ask questions and offer opinions.

Connection Prompts

Matthew is the kind of person who . . .

Matthew's mother is the kind of person who . . .

The barrel-shaped man is the kind of person who . . .

Murdoch is the kind of person who . . .

Murdoch's date is the kind of person who . . .

Write

Directions

1. *Review.* Go back to the Anticipation Guide that you partially completed on page 2. Read the statements and your responses in the Before Reading column. Do any of your responses seem questionable now, after you've read both excerpts from *The Rules of Survival?* If so, place a question mark next to those responses.

2. *Complete.* Choose a character from *The Rules of Survival* and write his or her name above the After Reading column. Imagine you are this character and complete the After Reading column as you think this character would most likely respond.

3. *Write.* On your own paper, write one or two paragraphs about secrets. Use the Anticipation Guide to fuel your ideas. For example, if you changed your mind about one or more responses after reading the selection and monitoring your understanding of it, explain what made you change your mind. If you think the response to an item depends on who you are and what situation you are in, explain why you think that. If you strongly agree or disagree with one or more items, explain why. Be sure to explain your reasons.

Reflections

Secrets

This chapter opened with an illustration of a girl who is about to learn another person's secrets. (See page 1.) Did you notice the smaller elements from this illustration scattered throughout the chapter?

What ideas did the main and smaller illustrations give you about secrets? How does this relate to your own experience sharing or uncovering secrets?

What did the excerpts from *The Rules of Survival* tell you about this issue?

Chapter 2

Equality

Seeing the Story

Think about books for young children. Such books rely heavily on pictures to tell the story. Some books for babies and very young children have no text at all.

As readers get older, they rely less and less on pictures to understand the story. They begin to use details in the text and their own imagination to create their own pictures in their minds. They personalize what they read, connecting or relating to the text in a unique way.

In this chapter, you'll learn more about how to connect to a text in your own way. To help you do this, you'll explore two reading strategies: **questioning the text** and **visualizing what the text describes**. Along the way, you'll be faced with some surprising ideas about equality and sameness.

Strategy ▶

Question the Text

Before You Read

(Word Grid)

Directions: Complete the following word grid for the word *equality*.

Step 1. Use a dictionary and thesaurus, if necessary, to complete the boxes for Definition, Synonyms, Divided into Syllables, and Antonyms.

Step 2. Use your own knowledge and ideas to list words that *equality* makes you think of (in Word Association), to give an Example of equality, to Use the Word in a Sentence, and to Sketch a simple drawing as a memory cue for the meaning of *equality*.

Sketch	Definition	Synonyms
	_____ _____ _____	_____ _____
Use the Word in a Sentence _____ _____ _____	**equality**	**Divided into Syllables** _____ _____ _____
Example _____ _____ _____	**Word Association** _____ _____ _____	**Antonyms** _____ _____ _____

Pros and Cons

Directions: With your teacher's guidance, form groups of four people. Together, complete the following steps.

Step 1. Write the word *equality* at the top of a sheet of paper. Then draw a line down the middle of the paper to make two columns. Label the left side Pros. Pros are things that are positive, or desirable about something. Label the right side Cons. Cons are things that are negative or undesirable about something.

Step 2. Working as a group, list as many pros and cons as you can for the idea of equality. To do so, ask questions about how the issue of equality affects your daily life—at home, in the community, at school, in the news and entertainment media, and so on.

Step 3. Regroup with the entire class to share your ideas in the larger group. Afterward, save your group's list of pros and cons. You'll use these lists later in this lesson.

While You Read

Reading Strategy Mini-Lesson

Reading Strategy ▶ Question the Text

Have you ever played one of those "What's Wrong with This Picture?" games? The idea is to find the details that are out of place. Maybe it's an orange hanging from an apple tree, mismatched shoes on someone's feet, or rain falling outside one window in a room while snow falls outside a nearby window. Just glancing at the picture, you may not notice these details.

Similarly, when you read a text you may not notice key details—unless you make an effort to notice them. And details, after all, help make a text pleasing and meaningful to read and reread.

In Chapter 1, you learned to ask yourself questions to monitor your understanding of a text. When you didn't understand something, you stopped to work out the meaning. Asking questions in this fashion helps when you are confused. You can take this strategy a step farther by **questioning the text** even when you are not confused. Questioning the text helps you notice key details that add meaning and interest—details that you may miss if you ask questions only when you're confused.

The table on the next page shows some types of questions that will help you notice meaningful details in what you read.

	Questioning the Text *To make sure I notice meaningful details*	
Question	**What It Helps You to Notice**	**Examples**
Who?	characters	Who are the key characters? Who is causing this problem? Who is speaking? Who did that?
What?	events problems or conflicts	What is this scene mostly about? What did that character just do? What is the main problem or conflict in the story? What started this argument?
When?	setting sequence of events	When does this scene take place? (past, present, future, day, night, etc.) When did a character do a specific action? When did he or she find out that information?
Where?	setting layouts of rooms, houses, buildings	Where does this scene take place? Where are the characters sitting/standing/walking in this scene?
Why?	causes and effects	Why did he or she do that? Why did he or she say that? Why did that happen?
How?	cause and effect similarities and differences solution or resolution	How did this problem begin? How do they know each other? How did he or she know that, or know how to do that? How is this character like/unlike that character? How did he or she solve the problem?

Watch This!

The Strategy in Action

In this table, you'll find a reading selection on the left. On the right is an example of how you can question the text to discover meaningful details.

Reading Selection	Question the Text
from Up From Slavery: An Autobiography by Booker T. Washington I was asked not long ago to tell something about the sports and pastimes that I engaged in during my youth. Until that question was asked it had never occurred to me that there was no period of my life that was devoted to play. From the time that I can remember anything, almost every day of my life has been occupied in some kind of labour; though I think I would now be a more useful man if I had had time for sports. During the period that I spent in slavery I was not large enough to be of much service, still I was occupied most of the time in cleaning the yards, carrying water to the men in the fields, or going to the mill, to which I used to take the corn, once a week, to be ground . . . I had no schooling whatever while I was a slave, though I remember on several occasions I went as far as the schoolhouse door with one of my young mistresses to carry her books. The picture of several dozen boys and girls in a schoolroom engaged in study made a deep impression	The first paragraph starts with "I." **Who** is "I"? The title tells me that this is an autobiography by Booker T. Washington. So "I" must be Booker. **Who** is Booker? He talks about being in slavery—he was a slave as a boy. **What** is this paragraph mostly about? It tells how Booker did a lot of work and never got to play as a kid. **Why** does this matter? Booker says he would be a more useful man if he had been able to play sports as a kid. **When** did these events happen? Booker talks about not being large enough to be of much service, so he must have been very young. But he doesn't give a year. It was during the time of slavery, obviously. **What** is this paragraph mostly about? It's about school. **What** is Booker's conflict? He never got to go to school. **How** did this make him feel? He envied the kids in school and wished he could go, too. **How** is Booker like the young mistress? They are both

Reading Selection *continued*	Question the Text *continued*
upon me, and I had the feeling that to get into a schoolhouse and study in this way would be about the same as getting into paradise.	school-aged, but only the mistress gets to go to school. That's so unfair and unequal. ***What*** is the "young mistress" like? She could carry her own books, but she has a slave child do it. ***Why*** does she do that? Booker doesn't say why; maybe it was a common thing to do.

Give It a Try

Question the Text

Directions: Draw a line down the center of a sheet of paper, making two columns. Label one column *What I Asked* and the other column *What My Question Helped Me Discover*. Keep this paper and a pencil handy and read the excerpt from the short story "Harrison Bergeron" on pages 26–29. While reading, write questions that you ask the text and note meaningful details that you discover. To review six useful question types, use the table on page 24.

Reading Selection

from **Harrison Bergeron**

by Kurt Vonnegut Jr.

The year was 2081, and everybody was finally equal. They weren't only equal before God and the law. They were equal every which way. Nobody was smarter than anybody else. Nobody was better looking than anybody else. Nobody was stronger or quicker than anybody else.

All this equality was due to the 211th, 212th, and 213th Amendments to the Constitution, and to the unceasing vigilance of agents of the United States Handicapper General.

Some things about living still weren't quite right, though. April, for instance, still drove people crazy by not being springtime. And it was in that clammy month that the H-G men took George and Hazel Bergeron's fourteen-year-old son, Harrison, away.

It was tragic, all right, but George and Hazel couldn't think about it very hard. Hazel had a perfectly average intelligence, which meant she couldn't think about anything except in short bursts. And George, while his intelligence was way above normal, had a little mental handicap radio in his ear. He was required by law to wear it at all times. It was tuned to a government transmitter. Every twenty seconds or so, the transmitter would send out some sharp noise to keep people like George from taking unfair advantage of their brains.

George and Hazel were watching television. There were tears on Hazel's cheeks, but she'd forgotten for the moment what they were about.

On the television screen were ballerinas.

A buzzer sounded in George's head. His thoughts fled in panic, like bandits from a burglar alarm.

"That was a real pretty dance, that dance they just did," said Hazel.

"Huh?" said George.

"That dance—it was nice," said Hazel.

"Yup," said George. He tried to think a little about the ballerinas. They weren't really very good—no better than anybody else would have been, anyway. They were burdened with sashweights[1] and bags of birdshot, and their faces were masked, so that no one, seeing a free and graceful gesture or a pretty face, would feel like something the cat drug in. George was toying with the vague notion that maybe dancers shouldn't be handicapped. But he didn't get very far with it before another noise in his ear radio scattered his thoughts.

George winced. So did two out of the eight ballerinas.

Hazel saw him wince. Having no mental handicap herself she had to ask George what the latest sound had been.

---

[1] sashweight: weight that balances another weight

"Sounded like somebody hitting a milk bottle with a ball peen hammer," said George.

"I'd think it would be real interesting, hearing all the different sounds," said Hazel, a little envious. "All the things they think up."

"Um," said George.

"Only, if I was Handicapper General, you know what I would do?" said Hazel. Hazel, as a matter of fact, bore a strong resemblance to the Handicapper General, a woman named Diana Moon Glampers. "If I was Diana Moon Glampers," said Hazel, "I'd have chimes on Sunday—just chimes. Kind of in honor of religion."

"I could think, if it was just chimes," said George.

"Well—maybe make 'em real loud," said Hazel. "I think I'd make a good Handicapper General."

"Good as anybody else," said George.

"Who knows better'n I do what normal is?" said Hazel.

"Right," said George. He began to think glimmeringly about his abnormal son who was now in jail, about Harrison, but a twenty-one gun salute in his head stopped that.

"Boy!" said Hazel, "that was a doozy, wasn't it?"

It was such a doozy that George was white and trembling and tears stood on the rims of his red eyes. Two of the eight ballerinas had collapsed to the studio floor, were holding their temples.

"All of a sudden you look so tired," said Hazel. "Why don't you stretch out on the sofa, so's you can rest your handicap bag on the pillows, honeybunch." She was referring to the forty-seven pounds of birdshot in canvas bag, which was padlocked around George's neck. "Go on and rest the bag for a little while," she said. "I don't care if you're not equal to me for a while."

George weighed the bag with his hands. "I don't mind it," he said. "I don't notice it any more. It's just a part of me."

"You been so tired lately—kind of wore out," said Hazel. "If there was just some way we could make a little hole in the bottom of the bag, and just take out a few of them lead balls. Just a few."

"Two years in prison and two thousand dollars fine for every ball I took out," said George. "I don't call that a bargain."

Remember to write down any questions you have as you read.

"If you could just take a few out when you came home from work," said Hazel. "I mean—you don't compete with anybody around here. You just set around."

"If I tried to get away with it," said George, "then other people'd get away with it and pretty soon we'd be right back to the dark ages again, with everybody competing against everybody else. You wouldn't like that, would you?"

"I'd hate it," said Hazel.

"There you are," said George. "The minute people start cheating on laws, what do you think happens to society?"

If Hazel hadn't been able to come up with an answer to this question, George couldn't have supplied one. A siren was going off in his head.

"Reckon it'd fall all apart," said Hazel.

"What would?" said George blankly.

"Society," said Hazel uncertainly. "Wasn't that what you just said?"

"Who knows?" said George.

Read-Aloud Opportunity ▶ Favorite Parts

Directions: Skim back over "Harrison Bergeron" on pages 26–29. Choose your favorite part of the story, such as a scene, a paragraph, or a conversation between characters. Then, with your teacher's guidance, form groups of four students. Each person reads aloud his or her favorite part of the story and explains why that part is appealing. In return, group members may make comments or ask questions about that part.

After You Read

 **Connect**

Directions

1. *Imagine.* Imagine what your life would be like if the agents of the Handicapper General truly had power in the United States. What would your life be like at home? At school? Think about a specific way your life would be different.

2. *Create.* With your teacher's guidance, form groups of four people. Share your ideas from step 1. Then use one or more of the ideas to write a short skit. (One person can act as recorder, with everyone suggesting dialogue and stage directions.) Practice the skit quietly.

3. *Perform.* Regroup with the entire class. Your teacher will organize a performance lineup. Perform your skit for the class.

Converse

Directions

1. *Rethink.* With your teacher's guidance, form the same groups that worked on the Pros and Cons activity on page 23. Take out your group's list of pros and cons. Discuss whether reading and questioning "Harrison Bergeron" made you rethink any of the pros or cons. Did any of the skits performed for the Connect activity on page 29 cause you to rethink your ideas?

2. *Modify.* Mark up the sheet of pros and cons. If you think an item should be removed as a pro or con, place an X next to the item. If you think an item should be moved to the other column (the pro now seems to be a con, for example), circle it and draw an arrow pointing to the other column. Place a question mark next to each item about which group members disagree. If you want to add a new pro or con, write it in the appropriate column and place a star beside it.

3. *Share.* Regroup with the entire class to share your new ideas with the larger group.

Write

Directions: Questioning a story helps you discover meaningful details. As a result, you gain a deeper understanding of the story. Which section of "Harrison Bergeron" is most meaningful to you (gave you something interesting to think about or helped you understand the story)? Perhaps it is a conversation between characters, or a scene with action, or the ending. Perhaps it is something else. Write an essay of about three paragraphs in which you

- identify a particular section of "Harrison Bergeron" that is meaningful to you

- explain why the section is meaningful

- give examples or reasons to support your ideas

Strategy ▶
Visualize What the Text Describes

In the first half of this chapter you learned how to question the text to discover meaningful details. This reading strategy not only helps you understand and remember a text better, but it also can help you form vivid mental images about the text. In the following section, you'll learn more about how to **visualize what the text describes**.

Before You Read

Visualizations

Directions: Read the following sentence, letting the words create a picture in your mind.

> When the bus stopped, a teenager crossed the street.

On the lines below, describe specifically what you "saw" when you pictured the bus, the teenager, and the street. What did these things look like to you?

The bus _____

_____

The teenager _____

_____

The street _____

_____

Now, with your teacher's guidance, share your mental images with the class. How are other people's mental pictures different from yours? Why do you think everyone visualized the text a bit differently, even though everyone read the exact same sentence?

Freewrite

Directions: Freewrite on the following questions for three to five minutes.

> How would society be different if people could change their appearance at the click of a button? Would you want to live in such a society?

While You Read

Reading Strategy Mini-Lesson

Reading Strategy ▶ Visualize What the Text Describes

This section began by asking you to create a mental picture based on a single sentence. Do you remember that sentence? You may not remember the exact wording, but you probably remember that the sentence mentioned a bus, a teenager, and a street. Because you visualized these things, you are able to remember them long after you read the words.

Pictures can be powerful memory tools. They can also delight the mind and fuel the imagination. The reading strategy of **visualizing what the text describes** uses your ability to create pictures in your mind. You use details in the text, along with your own ideas and experiences, to take mental snapshots of what the text describes. These mental snapshots can help you understand the text better, remember sequence of events, recall facts and details, take pleasure in reading, and much more.

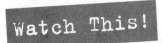

The Strategy in Action

In the left-hand column of the table that follows are the first five paragraphs of a chapter in *Uglies* by Scott Westerfeld. In the right-hand column is an example of how your thoughts may unfold as you visualize what the text describes.

Reading Selection	Visualize What the Text Describes
from **Uglies** by Scott Westerfeld "Here's option two." Tally touched her interface ring, and the wall-screen changed. This Tally was sleek, with ultrahigh cheekbones, deep green catlike eyes, and a wide mouth that curled into a knowing smile.	Hmm, interface ring and wallscreen sound like things from the future. But I can picture them. An interface ring would be like a computer mouse with buttons and a track ball, to interface with the computer screen—and it fits on the top

Reading Selection *continued*	Visualize What the Text Describes *continued*
"That's, uh, pretty different." "Yeah. I doubt it's even legal." Tally tweaked the eye-shape parameters, pulling the arch of the eyebrows down almost to normal. Some cities allowed exotic operations—for new pretties only—but the authorities here were notoriously conservative. She doubted a doctor would give this morpho a second glance, but it was fun to push the software to its limits. "You think I look too scary?" "No. You look like a real pussycat." Shay giggled. "Unfortunately, I mean that in the literal, dead-mouse-eating sense."	of a ring for your finger. I've seen girls wearing jewelry rings this big. I know what a computer screen looks like, and a wallscreen is probably just a big, flat computer screen hung on a wall. This description of Tally makes me think of Japanese anime art, or maybe comic book art. Everything is exaggerated. Shay's comment about Tally looking "like a real pussycat" makes me imagine a cat crossed with a person—a human body with cat ears, whiskers, and tiny nose.

Give It a Try

Visualize What the Text Describes

Directions: Read the complete excerpt from *Uglies* on pages 34–38 silently. As you read, make notes in the margin or on sticky notes describing the mental pictures that you visualize. Underline or write down words, phrases, or sentences in the text that are especially helpful. The tips on the next page may help you in this activity.

Tips for Visualizing

- Look for descriptions loaded with adjectives (words that describe people, places, or things). This is a sure clue that the writer is helping you visualize something.

- Watch for action. A simple verb (word that shows action) such as *shrugged* can inspire you to capture the moment in your mind.

- Imagine the expressions on characters' faces as they voice strong emotions.

- Look for sensory details—details that appeal to your sense of sight, hearing, touch, taste, or smell. This passage is especially rich in details that appeal to your sense of sight.

- Notice unusual words and use them to inspire a mental photo. For example, what do you picture when Shay calls Tally "Squint"?

Reading Selection

from Uglies
by Scott Westerfeld

"Here's option two." Tally touched her interface ring, and the wallscreen changed.

This Tally was sleek, with ultrahigh cheekbones, deep green cat-like eyes, and a wide mouth that curled into a knowing smile.

"That's, uh, pretty different."

"Yeah. I doubt it's even legal." Tally tweaked the eye-shape parameters, pulling the arch of the eyebrows down almost to normal. Some cities allowed exotic operations—for new pretties only—but the authorities here were notoriously conservative. She doubted a doctor would give this morpho a second glance, but it was fun to push the software to its limits. "You think I look too scary?"

"No. You look like a real pussycat." Shay giggled. "Unfortunately, I mean that in the literal, dead-mouse-eating sense."

"Okay, moving right along."

The next Tally was a much more standard morphological model, with almond-shaped brown eyes, straight black hair with long bangs, the dark lips set to maximum fullness.

"Pretty generic, Tally."

"Oh, come on! I worked on this one for a long time. I think I'd look great this way. There's a whole Cleopatra thing going on."

"You know," Shay said, "I read that the real Cleopatra wasn't even that great-looking. She seduced everyone with how clever she was."

"Yeah, right. And you've seen a picture of her?"

"They didn't have cameras back then, Squint."

"Duh. So how do you know she was ugly?"

"Because that's what historians wrote at the time."

Tally shrugged. "She was probably a classic pretty and they didn't even know it. Back then, they had weird ideas about beauty. They didn't know about biology."

"Lucky them." Shay stared out the window.

"So, if you think all my faces are so crappy, why don't you show me some of yours?" Tally cleared the wallscreen and leaned back on the bed.

"I can't."

"You can dish it out, but you can't take it, huh?"

"No, I mean I just can't. I never made one."

Tally's jaw dropped. Everyone made morphos, even littlies, too young for their facial structure to have set. It was a great waste of a day, figuring out all the different ways you could look when you finally became pretty.

"Not even one?"

"Maybe when I was little. But my friends and I stopped doing that kind of stuff a long time ago."

"Well." Tally sat up. "We should fix that right now."

"I'd rather go hoverboarding." Shay tugged anxiously under her shirt. Tally figured that Shay slept with her belly sensor on, hoverboarding in her dreams.

"Later, Shay. I can't believe you don't have a single morph. *Please*."

"It's stupid. The doctors pretty much do what they want, no matter what you tell them."

"I know, but it's *fun*."

Shay made a big point of rolling her eyes, but finally nodded. She dragged herself off the bed and plopped down in front of the wallscreen, pulling her hair back from her face.

Tally snorted. "So you have done this before."

"Like I said, when I was a littlie."

"Sure." Tally turned her interface ring to bring up a menu on the wallscreen, and blinked her way through a set of eyemouse choices. The screen's camera flickered with laser light, and a green grid sprang up on Shay's face, a field of tiny squares imposed across the shape of her cheekbones, nose, lips, and forehead.

Seconds later, two faces appeared on the screen. Both of them were Shay, but there were obvious differences: One looked wild, slightly angry, the other had a slightly distant expression, like someone having a daydream.

"It's weird how that works, isn't it?" Tally said. "Like two different people."

Shay nodded. "Creepy."

Ugly faces were always asymmetrical; neither half looked exactly like the other. So the first thing the morpho software did was take each side of your face and double it, like holding a mirror right down the middle, creating two examples of perfect symmetry. Already, both of the symmetrical Shays looked better than the original.

"So, Shay, which do you think is your good side?"

"Why do I have to be symmetrical? I'd rather have a face with two different sides."

Tally groaned. "That's a sign of childhood stress. No one wants to look at that."

"Gee, I wouldn't want to look stressed, "Shay snorted, and pointed at the wilder-looking face. "Okay, whatever. The right one's better, don't you think?"

"I *hate* my right side. I always start with the left."

"Yeah, well, I happen to like my right side. Looks tougher."

"Okay, You're the boss."

Tally blinked, and the right-side face filled the screen.

> **How do you picture this change?**

"First, the basics." The software took over: The eyes gradually grew, reducing the size of the nose between them, Shay's cheekbones moved upward, and her lips became a tiny bit fuller (they were already almost pretty-sized). Every blemish disappeared, her skin turning flawlessly smooth. The skull moved subtly under the features, the angle of her forehead tilting back, her chin becoming more defined, her jaw stronger.

When it was done, Tally whistled. "Wow, that's pretty good already."

"Great," Shay groaned. "I totally look like every other new pretty in the world."

"Well, sure, we just got started. How about some hair on you?" Tally blinked through menus quickly, picking a style at random.

When the wallscreen changed, Shay fell over on the floor in a fit of giggles. The high hairdo towered over her thin face like dunce cap, the white-blond hair utterly incongruous with her olive skin.

Tally could hardly manage to speak through her own laughter. "Okay, maybe not that." She flipped through more styles, settling on basic hair, dark and short. "Let's get the face right first."

She tweaked the eyebrows, making their arch more dramatic, and added roundness to the cheeks. Shay was still too skinny, even after the morpho software had pulled her toward the average.

"And maybe a bit lighter?" Tally took the shade of the skin closer to baseline.

"Hey, Squint," Shay said. "Whose face is this, anyway?"

"Just playing," Tally said. "You want to take a shot?"

"No, I want to go hoverboarding."

"Sure, great. But first let's get this right."

"What do you mean 'get it right,' Tally? Maybe I think my face is already right!"

"Yeah, it's great." Tally rolled her eyes. "For an ugly."

Shay scowled. "What, can't you stand me? Do you need to get some picture into your head so you can imagine it instead of my face?"

"Shay! Come on. It's just for fun."

"Making ourselves feel ugly is not fun."

"We *are* ugly!"

"This whole game is just designed to make us hate ourselves."

Tally groaned and flopped back onto her bed, glaring up at the ceiling. Shay could be so weird sometimes. She always had a chip on her shoulder about the operation, like someone was *making* her turn sixteen. "Right, and things were so great back when everyone was ugly. Or did you miss that day in school?"

"Yeah, yeah, I know," Shay recited. "Everyone judged everyone else based on their appearance. People who were taller got better jobs, and people even voted for some politicians just because they weren't quite as ugly as everybody else. Blah, blah, blah."

"Yeah, and people killed one another over stuff like having different skin color." Tally shook her head. No matter how many times they repeated it at school, she'd never really quite believed that one. "So what if people look more alike now? It's the only way to make people equal."

"How about making them smarter?"

Tally laughed. "Fat chance. Anyway, it's just to see what you and I will look like in only . . . two months and fifteen days."

"Can't we just wait until then?"

Tally closed her eyes, sighing. "Sometimes I don't think I can."

"Well, tough luck." She felt Shay's weight on the bed and a light punch on her arm. "Hey, might as well make the best of it. Can we go hoverboarding now? Please?"

Tally opened her eyes and saw that her friend was smiling. "Okay: hoverboard." She sat up and glanced at the screen. Even without much work, Shay's face was already welcoming, vulnerable, healthy . . . pretty. "Don't you think you're beautiful?"

Shay didn't look, just shrugged. "That's not me. It's some committee's idea of me."

Tally smiled and hugged her.

"It will be you, though. *Really* you. Soon."

Read-Aloud Opportunity ▶ Picture This!

Directions: With your teacher's guidance, form groups of three or four people. Look over the notes you made in "Give It a Try" on page 33. Find a section of text that inspired a strong picture in your mind. Read this section of text aloud to your group. Then describe your mental picture to the group. Point out words or phrases that helped you form the picture. Find out if other readers visualized a similar picture or imagined something quite different.

After You Read

Converse

Directions

1. *Plan.* With your teacher's guidance, form groups of five people. Together, write some questions that you would like to ask Tally, Shay, or another young person in the same situation. Then assign each person in your group a role: Talk Show Host, Tally, Shay, Young Person 3, or Young Person 4.

2. *Perform.* Regroup with the entire class, and your teacher will organize a performance schedule. Your group will stage a talk show performance for the rest of the class. The Talk Show Host asks questions to Tally, Shay, Young Person 3, and Young Person 4. They answer the questions, in character, expressing what they think their character would say and feel. The rest of the class plays the studio audience and may express feedback.

Connect

Directions: With your teacher's guidance, form groups of three or four people. Begin by having one person read aloud these quotations from the readings:

> The year was 2081, and everybody was finally equal. They weren't only equal before God and the law. They were equal every which way.
>
> —narrator in "Harrison Bergeron"

> "So what if people look more alike now? It's the only way to make people equal."
>
> —Tally in *Uglies*

Together, use details in the stories and your own ideas to answer the questions below. Record your answers in the table on the next page.

1. What does equality mean in "Harrison Bergeron"?

2. What does equality mean in *Uglies*?

3. What does equality mean to *me*?

Record your group's answers here.

What equality means . . .
in "Harrison Bergeron":
in *Uglies:*
to me:

 **Write**

Directions: Use details in *Uglies* and your own imagination to create a pamphlet about morphological software. (This is the software that Tally and Shay use in *Uglies* to morph, or change, their looks.) Your pamphlet should

- include at least two paragraphs that you write to promote the software as a good thing *or* criticize the software as undesirable
- include "before" and "after" images of Tally and/or Shay that you create using magazine cutouts or art supplies
- be targeted at young people ages 11 to 16

For creative ideas, you may want to look at pamphlets found in libraries, offices, or other places. Notice that pamphlets usually are laid out on folded paper and have a combination of text and images.

Reflections

Equality

This chapter opened with an illustration showing a person who doesn't fit in with a group of look-alike teens (See page 21.) Did you notice the small close-ups from this illustration scattered throughout the chapter?

What did the main and smaller illustrations tell you about equality and sameness? How does this relate to your own experience?

What ideas did the two readings give you about this issue?

Chapter 3

Expectations

Mapping It Out

Have you ever looked forward with excitement to seeing a movie or show on television? You heard about it, and maybe you saw previews for it. Maybe your friends told you about it. You planned when you would watch it, and you made sure you were there for the very first minute. Then, after five or ten minutes passed, you said to yourself, "This is not what I expected at all. How disappointing."

In this situation, you are free to leave the theater, or point the remote at the TV and click Off. You don't have to watch something that doesn't meet your expectations.

But what if a *person* doesn't meet your expectations? What if it is someone you love, or who loves you? You can't really point a remote at him or her and click Off, can you? Think about this problem as you work through this chapter. Along the way, you'll learn how to **identify main characters and main events** and **conflicts and resolutions** in stories.

Strategy▶
Identify Main Characters and Main Events

Before You Read

(Giving Advice)

Directions: People sometimes give advice by saying, "If I were you, I would . . ." Think about what advice a parent might give to a teen, using this type of sentence. What might a teen say to a parent? Write your ideas.

Parent to teen: If I were you, I would _____

_____

_____

Teen to parent: If I were you, I would _____

_____

_____

With your teacher's guidance, share your ideas with the class. Discuss why a parent or a teen might say what you wrote.

(Word Association)

Directions: Use the boxes on the next page to record your reactions to the words printed in them. First, in the box for "cradle," express ideas that the word *cradle* brings to your mind. You may write words, phrases, or even sentences. Next, repeat the process in the box for "hold." Finally, think about the two key words together—*cradle hold*—and use the third box to record your ideas about that phrase. You don't have to know the actual definition of the term yet; you'll figure that out as you read the selection. You're just recording your ideas about it for now.

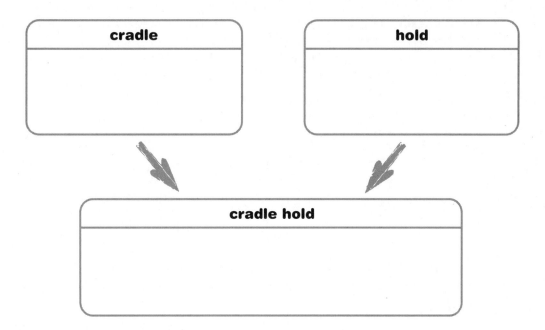

cradle	hold

cradle hold

While You Read

(Reading Strategy Mini-Lesson)

Reading Strategy ▶ Identify Main Characters and Main Events

Stories are made up of key elements, including setting, characters, and plot. *Big deal*, you may say. *All stories have a setting, one or more characters, and a plot. What's so important about that?*

Think of setting, characters, and plot as ingredients in a recipe. Every story has a similar list of ingredients, but the cook—or author—decides how to combine the ingredients, what "extras" to add, and how to present the finished product. This is the magic of storytelling. From the same set of ingredients come endless possibilities.

The reading strategy of **identifying main characters and main events** helps you discover how an author combined standard elements to create a unique narrative. This reading strategy helps you better understand the story. Also, you need to know the main characters and main events in order to figure out more complex aspects of a story, such as an unstated theme or a character's motivations.

A story has one or more ***characters***. Characters can be people, animals, or nonliving things like robots and talking toys. *Main characters* are the ones at the center of most of the action. Minor characters play supporting roles. Both types of characters contribute to attention-grabbing stories.

The table on the next page will help you identify main characters as you read.

Identifying Main Characters

1. As you read, make a list of the characters one by one, as they are introduced.
2. Make notes by the characters' names on their involvement in the story action.
3. Ask yourself, "Who is this story mostly about?"
4. Based on your notes and your answer to the question, identify the story's main characters.

Tips

- Often, the main character(s) are introduced first, then minor characters appear.
- The last scene in a story usually focuses on the main character(s).

A story's ***plot*** is made up of a series of actions or events. The action may be physical, such as learning to swim, or it may be mental, such as realizing a truth or making a decision.

The plot takes shape around a series of *main events*. In a story about a boy's sixth-grade year in school, a main event may be "Mike tries out for the baseball team." This single event is made up of many smaller actions. For example, Mike arrives for tryouts, argues with one of the other boys, plays ball, and talks to the coach afterward. Together, these actions make up one main event in the story. Main events move the story's plot forward.

Identifying Main Events

1. As you read the story, stop after every two or three paragraphs. Notice whether a series of smaller actions work together to form one key event.
2. If you get stuck, ask, "What main thing is happening to move the plot forward?"
3. As you read, list the main events in order. State the main action of each event.
4. Finally, review your list of events. Decide whether any events should be combined or whether you forgot an event.

Tips

- Some main events are told in just a few sentences or paragraphs. Others are told in many paragraphs.
- Often, main events are separated by a passage of time or a change of location in the story.

Watch This!

The Strategy in Action

Read "Prize Catch" on the next page. Following the selection is an example of how you might identify main characters and events in the story.

Prize Catch

"Dad! I caught a big one!" Phin shouted. He held tight to the line, feeling the pull from the other end.

"What'd I tell you, son?" Dad said. "That new bait really works!"

Phin struggled with the line. Slowly, he reeled it in. Every few seconds, the line would jerk and unspool. The water churned, stirring up mud from the lake bottom.

"I think you have an audience," Dad said.

Phin glanced behind him and saw at least five onlookers. Their faces were bright with anticipation. "Way to go!" shouted Gill, Phin's neighbor.

Dad chuckled. "Reel your catch in and show it off!"

With renewed effort, Phin reeled the line in, inch by inch. Whatever was caught on the hook was huge. As it came nearer, it thrashed and whipped about. A few whoops sounded from the onlookers.

Finally, the moment of victory arrived. The catch was inches in front of Phin's nose. He turned to look at his fans, basking in their delight.

"All right, son, you know what to do next," Dad said.

"Aw, Dad! Do I have to?" Phin whined. "Everybody's watching."

"It's the right thing to do—throw it back," Dad insisted.

"Oh, all right," Phin said. He unhooked the frightened human from his hook and flung it as hard as he could. The sopping wet man shot out of the lake, landing with a thump on the shore. Sucking in great gulps of air, the man said, "He threw me back! I'm alive!"

Identifying Main Characters in "Prize Catch"

Step	Notes
1. List the characters and describe their involvement in the plot.	Phin—first character mentioned in the story, does at least half of the talking, at the center of most of the action
	Dad—second character mentioned, is right there with Phin in most of the action and dialogue
	onlookers—briefly mentioned; mostly they watch Phin
	Gill—speaks once but is not needed to move the plot forward
	human—is not identified until the end, speaks once

Step *continued*	Notes *continued*
2. Who is "Prize Catch" mostly about?	The story is mostly about Phin and his dad. The onlookers are there, but they don't move the plot forward. Gill speaks once, but the action is not about him at all. Even though the human is important, he is not the focus of the action—the action focuses on Phin and Dad.
3. The main characters are . . .	Phin and Dad

Identifying Main Events in "Prize Catch"

Step	Notes
1a. Group a series of related actions into one main event. 1b. List the events. 1c. If you get stuck, ask, "What main thing is happening to move the plot forward?"	1. The first three paragraphs are about Phin reeling in a catch. 2. The next few paragraphs are about Phin enjoying the onlookers' delight. 3. After that, Phin struggles to get the catch reeled in. 4. In the end, Phin throws back the catch.
2. Review the list and make corrections, if necessary.	The onlookers' delight doesn't really move the plot forward. Maybe this part should be lumped in with the first event. Hmm, the events I listed as 1 and 3 are nearly identical—maybe I should combine them into one. Also, I left out the part about Phin arguing with his dad. It moves the plot forward, so I should list it as a main event.
3. The main events are . . .	1. Phin reels in a catch while enjoying the onlookers' delight. 2. Phin argues with Dad about throwing back the catch. 3. Phin throws back the catch.

Give It a Try

Identify Main Characters and Main Events

Directions: On your own, read "Cradle Hold" on pages 51–55. As you read, use the following two tables to record main characters and main events.

Identifying Main Characters in "Cradle Hold"

Step	Your Notes
1. List the characters and describe their involvement in the plot.	
2. Who is "Cradle Hold" mostly about?	
3. The main characters are . . .	

Identifying Main Events in "Cradle Hold"

Step	Your Notes
1a. Group a series of related actions into one main event. 1b. List the events. 1c. If you get stuck, ask, "What main thing is happening to move the plot forward?"	
2. Review the list and make corrections, if necessary.	
3. The main events are . . .	

Reading Selection

Cradle Hold

by David Klass

When Duke was five years old, Harry began to worry that his son was exhibiting too many feminine tendencies. Duke was small for his age, and he preferred dolls to guns and reading picture books to playing outdoors. Harry bought him a long plastic sword, which Duke tossed into the bottom of his playchest, and a two-headed ax, which Duke traded to the boy three houses down for a large stuffed pink elephant. When Harry saw the elephant, he decided that things had gone too far and that he'd better take matters into his own hands.

He took Duke to a football game, and the boy spent the entire time crawling around collecting bits of tinfoil that fans discarded on the bleachers as they finished their hot dogs. He brought home John Wayne movies on video and said, "See, that's who you're named after." But when he played them, Duke curled up into a little ball on the couch and promptly went to sleep.

Duke grew into a friendly but shy adolescent who kept pretty much to himself. He was particularly shy with girls. By the time Duke reached junior high school, Harry began noticing out loud that Duke spent every weekend studying and never went out on any dates. "You're only young once, you should be enjoying yourself," Harry told him. "Heck, if I had it to do over again . . ." Harry saw the look his wife threw him and stopped himself just in time. "I mean, you're a red-blooded American boy, and I want you to enjoy your salad days."

Harry began buying *Playboy* magazines and leaving them around the house, hoping his son would pick them up and page through them. Duke did occasionally leaf through them, but more often than not he read the articles and the interviews and ignored the pictorials.

When Duke was fourteen, they went on a family trip to Oceanside at the Jersey shore. It was a hot day in August, and the beach was packed. Harry suggested to Duke that they take a walk together. Harry had a tiny paunch, but his bright red-and-white Hawaiian bathing suit and the way he walked vigorously through the cold Atlantic surf gave him a carefree, youthful quality. Duke, on the other hand, wore conservative brown swim trunks and scampered out of the way of high-breaking waves. At fourteen and forty, Duke and Harry were almost exactly the same height, and except for the wrinkles around Harry's eyes and his almost completely bald pate, they might have been brothers.

As soon as they got out of earshot of his wife, Harry began making comments about the women they were passing. "Lookit those legs! Don't they get your motor goin'? Hey, getta load of that masterpiece." Finally, he stopped dead in his tracks. "Wow," he said, pointing. "We must have found heaven."

Four blond girls played a fast game of volleyball twenty yards away. All four of the girls were lovely-looking, and all of them wore tiny bikinis. "Whatta ya think of that?" Harry asked Duke. "How's that for a free show?"

"Can we go back now?" Duke mumbled.

"Go back? If I were you, I'd walk right up there and get in that game and meet those girls."

"Why don't you?"

"Don't be a smart-ass. I don't because I'm not you. But you're you. So what are you waiting for?"

"They have two teams. They don't need me."

"For Christ's sake," Harry said, "is something wrong with you?"

"No. Is something wrong with you?"

For a long moment father and son studied each other. Then Duke turned around and headed back towards his mother. Harry watched the blond girls play volleyball for a few more minutes, shook his head, and then headed back.

> **Remember to record all of the characters as you read.**

About a year after the trip to Oceanside, Duke got his first girlfriend. She was a quiet girl named Hillary, with a pretty smile and a talent for baking. For the first three months that they dated, Duke ate several meals a month with Hillary and her family, but he steadfastly refused to bring her home to meet his parents.

"Why? Is something wrong with them?" Hillary finally asked.

"Not really."

"So it's me?"

He kissed her. He had just learned that a kiss could be an acceptable answer to many of the difficult questions that crop up in a relationship. "Okay," he whispered, "if that's really what you want. But give me a week to get ready."

All that next week, at every opportunity, Duke warned Harry about what he would do if Harry didn't behave himself for Hillary's visit.

"What do you mean, behave myself? What the heck is that supposed to mean?"

"You know what it means."

"No, I don't."

"It means don't do anything weird. Don't say anything weird."

"What am I, some kind of creep?"

"Just don't."

"I won't. Whatever it is you mean."

Hillary showed up for dinner in a pretty blue dress that made her look adorable. Her hair was cut in neat bangs, she wore a pearl choker, and she brought a tin of pecan fudge brownies that she had baked herself.

Harry's face lit up when he first saw her. "Hey," he said, "welcome. More than welcome. I'm Harry. Duke's old man. You look great . . ."

Harry's wife immediately led Hillary away into the kitchen before Harry had a chance to say anything else to her. Harry was left in the living room, looking at Duke.

"Don't," Duke said. "Please."

"I don't know what you're talking about."

"I'll leave. And I won't come back."

Harry straightened up at the threat and looked carefully across the living room at his son. "Okay, but you can't stop me from thinking how proud I am of you."

"You can think whatever you want," Duke told him. "But if you say one thing to her, I'm out the door."

Harry was a perfect gentleman all evening. He treated Hillary with polite, restrained hospitality, carried on his share of the dinner table conversation amiably, and did not insist that Duke eat his roast beef blood rare.

The next day in the post office, Harry let loose. "You should see my boy's babe," he told Frank Wells when they were sorting the local mail.

Frank Wells was a short black man with a neat mustache. He was the only man in the post office who put up with Harry, because Harry occasionally gave him horse-racing tips that paid off. "Nice?"

"They didn't make girls like that when we were young."

"Lucky kid."

"I don't know about lucky, but he landed a beauty queen. Like a tall glass of lemonade on a hot day." Harry licked his lips. "Know what I mean?"

Frank shrugged. "You're screwing up those letters."

"To heck with the letters. I'm telling you, that kid has got his little piece of heaven. What do you think, Franky? Kinda hurts to grow old when you see something like that sitting down across from you at your dinner table."

"Hey, watch what you're saying," Frank told him, moving a half step away. "That's your son's girlfriend."

"Yeah," Harry said proudly, "I know." And in a different, sadder voice, he repeated, "I know."

> **What are the main events in this part?**

Later that year, Duke surprised and delighted his father by going out for the high-school wrestling team. He was still a thin and gawky kid—more elbows than shoulders and it looked for a long time as though he was going to be cut, but he went to all the practices and called Coach Waterman "sir," and ended up making the junior varsity as a substitute at 135 pounds.

Harry didn't miss a single wrestling match all season. Some of the junior varsity matches were held in tiny gyms in junior high schools and even elementary schools, and the team's bus driver often got lost trying to find his way to the right little school, but when the bus finally did pull to a stop, Harry's lime green Mercury Comet was always sitting in the parking lot.

Duke began slowly as a high-school wrestler, but in his sophomore year he started on the junior varsity, and between his sophomore and junior seasons he suddenly blossomed into a powerhouse. Other kids on the team worked out during the off-season and merely stayed in shape—each time Duke worked out, new muscles seemed to sprout on his calves, arms, shoulders, and back. Coach Waterman took one look at Duke's definition on the first day of preseason of his junior year and put him with the varsity team. "I think you've got a good chance of challenging for a starting spot," he told Duke. "Let's work your butt off in preseason and see what happens."

What happened was that Duke won a starting place on the varsity squad and finished out the season with a twelve-and-four record.

Harry came to every single match and shouted himself hoarse. Sometimes Harry sat next to Hillary, and as he screamed and punched the air, she twisted a little white handkerchief in her hands. When Duke won and the referee held his arm up in victory, Harry's face lit up brighter and brighter till it seemed ready to explode, like a star going supernova. On the rare occasions when Duke lost, Harry retreated into sullen depressions and refused to say a word for days on end.

to be continued

Read-Aloud Opportunity ▶ Teacher-Student Shared Reading

Directions: In this activity, the teacher alternates with students to read aloud "Cradle Hold" on pages 51–55. Here is the pattern to follow:

> **Teacher:** first paragraph
> > **Student 1:** second paragraph
>
> **Teacher:** third paragraph
> > **Student 2:** fourth paragraph
>
> **Teacher:** fifth paragraph
> > **Student 3:** sixth paragraph
>
> . . . and so on to finish the selection

After You Read

 Converse

Directions

1. *Organize.* With your teacher's guidance, form groups of two to six people. Your teacher will give each group an index card with a scene from "Cradle Hold" noted on it. Talk with the other groups to arrange the scenes in the order in which they happen in "Cradle Hold." Number your group's card so you know your place in the lineup.

2. *Create.* With your group members, create a tableau of the scene on your index card. A tableau (pronounced tah-bloh) is a grouping of people to form a scene, like a picture. The idea is to arrange yourselves to show the most important idea of the scene, including body positions and facial expressions. You hold the position as if you are frozen in a painting.

3. *Perform.* Finally, the groups perform their tableaux, in chronological order.

 **Connect**

Directions: Think about the first half of "Cradle Hold," on pages 51–55. In particular, think about Duke and Harry. What if Harry were your dad? What if *you* were Duke's mom or dad? On the lines below, write what you would do in each of these positions. Be sure to tell why you would do this (*hint*: use a word or phrase such as *because, since, in order to,* or *so that*). Your teacher may give you the opportunity to share your ideas with the class.

1. If Harry were my dad, I would _____

    _____

    _____

    _____

2. If I were Duke's mom or dad (circle one), I would _____

    _____

    _____

    _____

 **Write**

Directions: Each item that follows contains a character's name. On a scale below the name are two opposite character traits. Decide whether the character is described equally well by each trait or is more one trait than the other. Write an X on the scale to show where you place the character in relation to the traits. Then, on the lines provided, explain your choice. Use details from the story or your own experience and knowledge to make the explanation clear.

Example:

Hillary is . . .

traditional   modern

```
—+———⊁———+———+———+———+———+—
```

Explanation: *Hillary is a very traditional girl. For one thing, she likes to bake. Also, she wears a dress that makes her look "adorable," her bangs are "neat," and she wears pearls. She carries a "little white handkerchief" to Duke's games. All these things are traditional.*

1.   Duke is . . .

feminine   masculine

```
—+———+———+———+———+———+———+—
```

Explanation:_____

_____

_____

_____

2.   Duke is . . .
weak   strong
—|———————|———————|———————|———————|———————|———————|—

Explanation:_____

_____

_____

_____

3.   Harry is . . .
likable   unlikable
—|———————|———————|———————|———————|———————|———————|—

Explanation:_____

_____

_____

_____

4.   Harry is . . .
caring   selfish
—|———————|———————|———————|———————|———————|———————|—

Explanation:_____

_____

_____

_____

Strategy▶

Identify Conflict and Resolution

Read this short exchange of instant messages between two friends.

bballfan: what's up?
aim2win: hate my life
bballfan: why
aim2win: BFF dumped me for new friend
bballfan: ouch, what now?
aim2win: do u need a new BF?

In just a few short lines, bballfan and aim2win have identified a **conflict**: aim2win's best friend forever has lost interest in her and has gotten close to a new friend. Bballfan and aim2win have also identified a **solution**: aim2win suggests that she and bballfan become new best friends.

This example is a short version of what you'll see in most stories that you read. One or more characters will face a conflict and will have to solve it somehow. In the following lesson, you'll learn how to **identify conflict and resolution** in stories.

Before You Read

Make a Prediction

Directions: Read this description of the cradle, a wrestling technique.

> The *cradle* is a technique in amateur wrestling. A wrestler wraps one arm around the neck of his opponent. He hooks his other arm behind one knee of his opponent. He then joins his two hands together in a tight lock. The wrestler locked in this hold finds it very difficult to escape. If he finally does escape, he has used up valuable energy to do so. As a result, he may be more easily defeated. The term *cradle* is used because this technique is somewhat like the way a baby is cradled in one's arms.

Knowing that "Cradle Hold" is the title of the story you are reading, and knowing that the cradle is a wrestling technique, how do you think the story will end? Write your ideas on the lines below.

My prediction for how "Cradle Hold" will end: _____

_____

_____

_____

_____

Share a Memory

Directions: Has someone ever done something "nice" for you that ended up annoying, angering, or embarrassing you? Maybe your grandmother knits you strange-looking sweaters that you have to wear to family events. Or maybe a not-so-close friend calls you three times a day just to say hello. When we talk about these people, we often say, "She [he] means well, but . . ."

With your teacher's guidance, gather in small groups. In your group, share an experience in which someone meant well, but the results were not so great. Talk about whether it's the good intentions or the actual results that matter. Then share your ideas with the class.

While You Read

Reading Strategy Mini-Lesson

Reading Strategy ▶ Identify Conflict and Resolution

As you learned earlier in this chapter, a story has one or more characters and a series of main events. How do these elements fit together to form a story that grabs your attention and keeps you reading to the end? They are shaped by a **conflict** and a **resolution**.

The *conflict* is the main problem that the main character must solve. In "Prize Catch," Phin's problem is trying to reel in a catch that struggles and fights back. Most of the story focuses on this challenge.

Each main event in a story shows you something new about the conflict. Usually, the main events create tension or suspense about the conflict. You begin to wonder, How will the character solve this problem? Or get out of this mess? Or survive this situation?

The kinds of conflict that characters face are limited only by writers' imaginations. But most types of conflict are one of the four below.

Type of Conflict	Explanation	Example
Character versus character	Conflict/challenge comes from another character.	In *Eleven* by Laura Myracle, Winnie grows apart from her best friend.
Character versus self	Conflict/challenge is internal (inside) the character.	In *Olive's Ocean* by Kevin Henkes, Martha must deal with big changes in her life.
Character versus society	Conflict/challenge comes from what society says is right and wrong versus your own values.	In *The Giver* by Lois Lowry, Jonas confronts his community's attempt to create a pain-free society.

Type of Conflict *continued*	Explanation *continued*	Example *continued*
Character versus nature	Conflict/challenge comes from an animal or natural force.	In *Hatchet* by Gary Paulsen, Brian must survive alone in the wilderness after a plane crash.

Knowing the basic types of conflict helps when you identify the conflict in a specific story. You can also ask questions that help you identify the conflict.

Identifying the Conflict in a Story

To identify the conflict, ask

- What is the challenge that the main character faces?
- What is keeping the main character from reaching his or her goal?
- What is making life difficult for the main character?

The *resolution* is the solution, or outcome, to the problem. In "Prize Catch," Phin's problem is not solved when he reels the catch in close. He still must decide what to do with the catch. The resolution is Phin's decision to throw the catch back.

The resolution usually unfolds in just one or two main events near or at the end of the story. To identify a story's resolution, pay special attention to what happens near the end. You can also ask these helpful questions:

Identifying the Resolution in a Story

To identify the resolution, ask

- How is the conflict resolved or stopped?
- Why does the problem stop being a problem?

Watch This!

The Strategy in Action

The following table shows an example of how your thoughts may unfold as you identify the conflict and the resolution in "Prize Catch."

Identifying Conflict and Resolution in "Prize Catch"

Step	Your Notes
1. Ask—and answer—questions to identify the conflict. • What is the challenge that Phin faces? • What is keeping Phin from reaching his goal? • What is making life difficult for Phin?	Phin is challenged by trying to reel in the catch, which is fighting back on the fishing line.
2. State the conflict.	The conflict for Phin is trying to reel in a catch.
3. Ask—and answer—questions to identify the resolution. • How is the conflict resolved or stopped? • Why does Phin's problem stop being a problem?	The conflict ends when Phin decides to throw back the catch. Once he throws back the human, there is no more problem.
4. State the resolution.	The resolution to Phin's problem is throwing back the catch.

Give It a Try

Identify Conflict and Resolution

Directions: Read the second half of "Cradle Hold," on pages 62–69. Then use the table on the next page to help you identify the main conflict and the resolution in both halves of the story.

Identifying Conflict and Resolution
in "Cradle Hold"

Step	Your Notes
1. Ask—and answer—questions to identify the main conflict. • What is the challenge that Duke faces? • What is keeping Duke from reaching his goal? • What is making life difficult for Duke?	
2. State the conflict.	
3. Ask—and answer—questions to identify the resolution. • How is the conflict resolved or stopped? • Why does Duke's problem stop being a problem?	
4. The resolution in "Cradle Hold" is . . .	

Reading Selection

Cradle Hold

by David Klass

continued from page 55

Duke's senior season lived up to expectations. His speed was such that at the beginning of a match he could shoot in for a single- or even a double-leg takedown, and even when his opponents knew he was coming, they couldn't do much to stop him. As soon as he had a controlling position, he'd slap on a cross-face or hook a leg and work right for the pin. Many of his matches ended in the first period, and the *Bergen Record* made him "Athlete of the Week" in February.

The county high-school wrestling championships were held in the large Edgewood High School gym. The winners of the county championship at each weight class would go on to the state tournament, so there was a lot at stake. A cable TV station broadcast all the matches, and more than a dozen sports reporters hung around the tournament following the progress of the favorites.

Duke was seeded second in the county, behind Bankman of Hackensack, who had won the title the previous year. On the first three days of the tournament, Duke and Bankman waltzed through their preliminary and quarterfinal and semifinal matches, and neither of them was even pushed. Harry took the days off from work and always sat in the center of the second row of bleachers, screaming for Duke during his matches and studying Bankman carefully when the Hackensack grappler was on the mats.

The night before the county final, during dinner, Harry tried to advise Duke. "It's the damn cradle that makes him so dangerous. He's got more ways of working someone into that cradle than a dog has fleas. Once he gets it, or even a half cradle, or even a cross-face, it's goodbye, Charlie. Take my advice, and—"

Duke put down his fork. "What do you know about wrestling?" he asked, cutting his father off. "Have you ever wrestled?"

Harry's wife, who was eating peas with a spoon, paused between scoops to wait for her husband's answer. Her face seemed to be blank, yet Harry read a tiny, sarcastic smile in the turn of her lips. Harry frowned at her and then looked back at Duke. "No, I've never wrestled, but I've seen enough to have picked up a few things."

"Just don't talk about tomorrow," Duke said. "Whatever happens is gonna happen, and I don't want to think about it."

"You're gonna win. You're gonna pin that clown."

Duke stood up from the table. "I said don't talk about it."

"I just wanted to tell you to be aware of that cradle hold. I won't say any more—"

The fury in Duke's voice surprised everyone at the table as he half shouted, "You have no idea. None at all. Do you know what it's like out there on the mat when the ref blows the whistle and it's just you and some other guy, trying to pin each other, and hundreds of people watching?

> **Identify the conflicts as you read.**

Do you know what it's like to be tied up and pinned, to be put on your back and held there? A cradle's the worst—you can't straighten out, your own strength is useless, it's a nightmare . . . you have no idea."

"I was just trying to make a suggestion," Harry mumbled.

"Well, don't."

Harry's mumble sank down to a whisper. "I just want to see you win tomorrow."

The anger stayed in Duke's voice, but his eyes softened the tiniest bit as he growled, "I know you do."

The state final match at 135 pounds was the only county final that pitted two undefeated wrestlers against each other. As Duke and Bankman walked onto the mat, the crowd rewarded them for their outstanding seasons with a burst of applause. The two young wrestlers eyed each other. Bankman was two inches shorter than Duke, with black hair that he wore in a military-style crew cut and a long scar that stretched from his nose to his left ear. As soon as he graduated from high school he planned to join the U.S. Marines.

Harry sat in his usual spot in the second row. On this final day of the tournament, his wife sat next to him, and as he watched his son and Bankman, he made dozens of excited observations to her. "See the way Bankman walks—his feet never lift, they just slide. See, even just standing still, he keeps his hands in close to his body. Duke's got better technique, but that cradle scares the heck outta me. Up, there they go . . . *C'mon, Duke!*"

The first period seesawed back and forth for several minutes. Bankman started off in the control position, but Duke wrestled carefully and soon engineered a neat escape. They circled in the center of the mat, and then Duke shot in for a leg and took Bankman down hard. Harry jumped to his feet and punched the air with both fists. *"C'mon, Duke, pin that clown. Pin him."*

For more than a minute, Duke stayed in control, trying to set up a pinning combination. Near the end of the first period he got a bit overeager and careless, and Bankman pulled off a stunning reversal. Suddenly Duke was on the bottom and Bankman was on top, and the wrestler from Hackensack brought his arms around in a flash and clamped on a cradle hold.

The large crowd roared as Bankman went for the pin. The ref got down on his knees, watching Duke's shoulders as Duke rocked back and forth and strained and tried to bridge with his head and neck.

Harry was standing and punching the air with both fists when he suddenly realized that Bankman had pulled a masterful reversal. Harry's fists slowly unclenched, but he never lowered his arms. He watched Duke's desperate efforts to resist the pin, saw that there was still more than a minute left in the period and Duke would never make it, and then he started moving forward.

Harry's wife grabbed for his arm but missed. As soon as Harry was down on the floor of the gym, he raced straight for the mats. The roar of the crowd swelled in his ears, and his eyes were fixed on his son's shoulders, which were being forced down slowly but inexorably.

When Harry reached the two wrestlers, he hooked his right arm under Bankman's jaw and his left hand under his stomach and tried to yank the Hackensack wrestler off. Bankman resisted and then yielded, more out of confusion than necessity. He thought that it had to be the referee trying to pull him off and that his opponent must have given up or lost consciousness.

As soon as Bankman let go of Duke, Harry released him. The referee, Harry, and Bankman stood looking at each other as Duke got up on one knee and recognized his father.

"What are you, crazy?" the referee asked Harry.

Harry couldn't think of anything to say. He looked down at his son, who was glaring back up at him with more anger than it seemed possible for a human face to contain. Without a word, Harry turned and hurried toward the rear exit. The crowd had grown quiet, and nobody made a move to stop Harry as he disappeared out the back door of the gym.

"Do you know that guy? Is he with your team? Should we get the police after him?" the ref asked Duke in rapid fire.

Duke stood up. "Don't get the police."

"I'm gonna have to talk to the judges, but I think he should win on a forfeit," the ref said to Duke.

"Absolutely." Duke held out his right hand to Bankman. "Congratulations."

"Thanks," Bankman said, still very confused. "Who the heck was that idiot?"

Duke shrugged, turned, and walked off the mats. He didn't go home till late that night. When he walked through the door, his mother, looking nervous, got up from the living room armchair. "Thank God you're home," she said.

"Why?" Duke said.

"I've been worried about your father."

At the mention of his father, Duke felt his body tense with fury from his jaw to the bottoms of his feet. "Where is he?"

She pointed out the front door.

"I didn't see him when I came in."

"He's walking around the block."

"What do you mean, he's walking around the block? What's he doing?"

"Just walking," she said.

"How long has he been out there?"

"Since the wrestling meet. I tried to talk to him, but he just kept walking."

Without another word, Duke walked out of the living room, through the hall, and out the front door. He waited halfway up the walk, and sure enough, within five minutes he made out his father's figure walking quickly through the gloom. When his father saw him, he slowed momentarily and then resumed his pace.

Duke walked the rest of the way out to the sidewalk. Harry reached him and hurried right by him without saying a word. "Hey," Duke said. *"Hey."* He ran after Harry and fell into step alongside him. "Is this a stunt or what? Are you trying for sympathy? Do you want us all to think you're completely crazy? Is that the game now?"

"I'm just walking," Harry said.

"Do you realize what you did today? Do you know how hard I worked for that chance at the county title? Of course you do."

"I owe you an apology," Harry said. "I'm sorry."

"An apology? What good is an apology?" They rounded the corner onto Chestnut Street, never slackening pace for a moment.

"Everyone on the team thinks you're insane. Mom thinks so too. Coach Waterman wanted to try to have you arrested."

"I don't know what to say," Harry said.

"Why don't you start by saying something true," Duke told him, "and we'll take it from there. Say one true thing about what happened today and what's going on."

Harry stopped walking. He was breathing a bit hard. "I love you," he said. "You're my boy and I love you."

Duke ground his knuckles together in fury. "Why did you do that?"

"I couldn't let him pin you. I just couldn't."

"Well, I just can't take it anymore."

"You're leaving?"

"For a while," Duke said. "I'm gonna stay with a guy on the team. Al Gordon. His parents have a big house with a spare room. They said it would be okay."

"They're nice folks, to put you up like that," Harry said. He began walking again, more slowly this time. Duke walked with him.

"I wish I could understand you. I wish you'd at least try. I think you owe me that."

"Do you know what I do all day?" Harry asked. "I sort mail into bins."

"Don't try to turn your career into a sob story. It's a good job."

"Maybe it is, but you asked and I'm trying to answer. I sort mail into big gray metal bins. And I think about you." Harry paused and inhaled the cold, clear air of the suburban New Jersey night. "You never knew this, but before you were born, we decided we were going to call you Herbert. But when I saw you for the first time, I thought of John Wayne and I changed it in a flash to Duke . . ." His voice dropped off. "You don't know what it's like to sort mail. And you don't know . . ." Harry was silent for a long minute. "You don't know what it's like not to be eighteen years old."

"That's an explanation?"

"Who says there has to be a good explanation for everything? That's the most I can say."

"It's nonsense," Duke said.

"Maybe it is."

They turned onto Grove Street and headed for home. Their footsteps rang together, sounding with almost perfect symmetry. "At least he didn't pin you," Harry finally said with the thinnest of smiles.

"That's true. He didn't pin me."

"Walk with me one more time around the block?" Harry asked. "We don't have to talk. Just walk with me. Even if you hate me."

They reached their house, and Duke slowed down and hesitated. Then he sped up again and rejoined Harry. They passed the Greenfields' flagstone driveway and the Murdochs' overgrown front yard, which was the disgrace of the block, and Mr. Beeman waved to them from the rocker on his winterized front porch. They passed the bus stop on the corner, and the mail box where Duke had cut his forehead when he was ten, and the stoplight.

"I don't hate you," Duke muttered from between tight lips.

Harry glanced sideways at his son. "Nice night."

"Getting cold."

Is there a resolution? Why or why not?

"Ring around the moon. Rain tomorrow."

"More likely snow."

"You looked good out there today," Harry told him. "Bankman's tough, but you were beating him. Breaks didn't go your way."

"That cradle hold's one of the toughest to break," Duke muttered, glancing at his father. The mixed emotions in his voice almost choked him. "Once it's clamped on there's no real way out."

Harry nodded. "What can I say? For me too. You'll do better with your kid. Anyway, you looked good."

"Thanks. We're almost at the house. I should go now."

"To Al Gordon's?"

"Yes. His parents are probably waiting up for me. You should go in to Mom. She's worried."

"I will," Harry promised. "I think I'm gonna just take one more turn around the block and then I'll go in. Join me?"

"It's too cold. My nose is getting numb. Goodbye. I'll call you or something."

They both stopped walking and stood facing each other. Suddenly Harry stepped forward and reached out with both arms, and before Duke could react, he was wrapped up in the first embrace he had ever received from his father. He didn't know what to do. He didn't try to break away. He also didn't hug Harry back. Instead, Duke stood there stiffly in the cold night, feeling his father's hands clasping together around the small of his back, and waited for his father to release him.

Read-Aloud Opportunity ▶ Teacher-Student Shared Reading

Directions: Read aloud the second half of "Cradle Hold" (on pages 62–69), just as you did the first half—by alternating between teacher and student. Here is the pattern to follow:

> **Teacher:** first paragraph
> > **Student 1:** second paragraph
> **Teacher:** third paragraph
> > **Student 2:** fourth paragraph
> **Teacher:** fifth paragraph
> > **Student 3:** sixth paragraph
> . . . and so on to finish the selection

After You Read

 **Converse**

Directions

1. *Think.* Review your responses in the Write activity on page 56. Now that you have finished reading "Cradle Hold," would you change where you placed the Xs on Duke's and Harry's scales in the activity? Think about why you would or wouldn't change each scale.

2. *Share.* With your teacher's guidance, form small groups. Begin with the first item in the Write activity. Group members share their first responses to that item with the group and discuss whether they would change the location of the X. One by one, discuss all four items.

 **Connect**

Directions: Imagine that you write an advice column for your school newspaper. One day, you get a letter from a student named Duke. His letter describes the conflict he is having with his dad, Harry. He tells you about many of the events in "Cradle Hold." Then he asks you to suggest a solution to his problem.

On your own paper, write Duke's letter. Then team up with a partner and swap letters. Write a response back to your partner's letter from Duke. In one or two paragraphs, tell him

- how you think he should solve his problem
- why you think your solution will work

 **Write**

Directions: Choose option A or B.

    A. Imagine that Duke takes the advice that you gave him in the Connect activity, above. Write a new ending for "Cradle Hold" that shows how Duke takes your advice and creates a solution to his problem.

    OR

    B. Write a continuation of "Cradle Hold," either one month later, six months later, or a year later.

Whether you pick A or B, make sure that you include

- the main characters and, if you want, one or more minor characters
- at least one main event
- dialogue (conversation between characters)

Reflections

Expectations

This chapter opened with an illustration of a competitive situation in which expectations are running high. (See page 43.) Did you notice the close-ups from this illustration scattered throughout the chapter?

What did the main and smaller illustrations tell you about expectations? What do others expect of you? What are your expectations for yourself?

What ideas did the readings give you about when these expectations clash?

4

Embarrassing Moments

Telling What Happened

Suppose you and a friend have been planning to attend a basketball game together. At the last minute, your friend gets sick. You have to go alone, but you promise that later you'll tell your friend what happened at the game. What will your friend most want to know?

Most likely, you'll tell your friend about key players, exciting plays, memorable moments, and the final score. In other words, you will summarize the game, including the most important details.

If you've ever described a game, a party, or a movie to a friend, then you have some practice in recalling key details and summarizing what happened. This chapter will help you polish those skills. As you read "Last Dance," a short story about a girl's embarrassing moment, you'll learn to **recall story details** and **summarize a story**. These skills are especially useful for understanding and remembering what you read.

71

Strategy▶
Recall Story Details

Before You Read

(Word Table)

Directions: Use this word table to prepare for reading "Last Dance" on pages 77–80. The first column lists a challenging word from the passage. In the second column, write the meaning of the word. In the third column, come up with a memory cue, such as a sketch or phrase, to help you remember the word's meaning. The first one has been done for you as an example. Using a dictionary or other resource, fill in the information for the remaining words.

Word	Meaning	Memory Cue
flush (v)	blush; turn red from embarrassment	☺
colossal (adj)		
drab (adj)		
cringe (v)		
clammy (adj)		
reverie (n)		

Preview the Passage

Directions: Read the title and first three paragraphs of the passage beginning on page 77. Then jot down your reactions to the parts of the passage listed in the table below. At the bottom of the table, write your best guess of what the story will be about. Your teacher may ask you to share your ideas with your classmates.

Part of Passage	Your Thoughts or Expectations of the Story, Based on this Part
Story title	
First and second paragraphs	
Third paragraph	
My best guess of what the story will be about, based on the clues above:	

While You Read

Reading Strategy Mini-Lesson

Reading Strategy ▶ Recall Story Details

Sporting events, concerts, plays, monster truck races—you can watch them all from a seat in the stands. Whether you sit in the first few rows or way in the back, you can see and hear what happens. However, if you've ever witnessed one of these events, you know that you can see more if you sit up close. You can see the details, and the details make your experiences more vivid, more delightful, more memorable. This is one reason why tickets for front-row seats cost the most.

In Chapter 3, you learned to identify main characters, events, conflict, and resolution in a story. That was the big picture, the one you can see sitting way in the back. In this lesson, you will learn to notice and **recall story details**—these are the parts that you see when you get up close: the dragon tattoo on the tough guy's arm, the hairy wart on the old lady's nose, the way the love-struck teenager blushes when a certain girl comes near. The main parts of a story give it shape, like a skeleton. But the *details* make the story worth front-row seating.

One of the most helpful ways to organize facts and details about main parts of a story is to use a graphic organizer like this one.

Main Part 1	**Main Part 2**
List a character, setting, event, or idea from the story.	*List a character, setting, event, or idea from the story.*
Details	**Details**
List details about the part of the story you listed above.	*List details about the part of the story you listed above.*

Title

Write the story title here.

Main Part 3	**Main Part 4**
List a character, setting, event, or idea from the story.	*List a character, setting, event, or idea from the story.*
Details	**Details**
List details about the part of the story you listed above.	*List details about the part of the story you listed above.*

By listing a story's main parts and key details in an organizer like this, you are forced to be observant. You must notice not only "Who is important?" or "What is happening?" but also "What makes this person come alive on the page?" and "What makes me feel as if I am right there in this event?"

Watch This!

The Strategy in Action

You may be familiar with the movie *Spider-Man*. The following graphic organizer shows how you can organize facts and details about main parts of this story.

Main Part 1

(character) Peter Parker

Details

- *nerdy, awkward*
- *bullied at school*
- *photographer for school newspaper*
- *gains spiderlike abilities*

Main Part 2

(character) Norman Osborn

Details

- *very wealthy*
- *takes drug*
- *has alter ego, Green Goblin*
- *Spider-Man's enemy*
- *son is Peter's friend Harry*

Title

Spider-Man

Main Part 3

(setting) New York

Details

- *Queens*
- *Manhattan*
- *skyscrapers*

Main Part 4

(event) Peter gets bitten by spider and becomes Spider-Man.

Details

- *on school trip*
- *radioactive spider runs away*
- *Peter gets bitten*
- *gains strength and ability to shoot webs and climb things*
- *gains ability to sense danger*

Give It a Try

Recall Story Details

Directions: Read the first half of the story "Last Dance" on pages 77–80. As you read, use the following graphic organizer to write facts and details about the parts of "Last Dance" listed in the boxes.

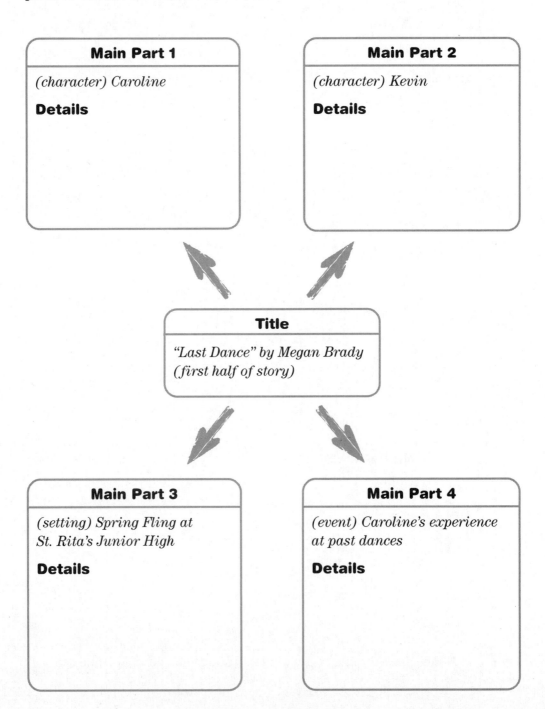

Main Part 1

(character) Caroline

Details

Main Part 2

(character) Kevin

Details

Title

"Last Dance" by Megan Brady (first half of story)

Main Part 3

(setting) Spring Fling at St. Rita's Junior High

Details

Main Part 4

(event) Caroline's experience at past dances

Details

Reading Selection

Last Dance

by Megan Brady

Caroline stood at the edge of her junior high's gym floor, fiddling with the charm on her necklace. Most of the time she didn't even realize she was fiddling—it was just what she did when she was nervous. And she was very nervous tonight. Kevin Harris was on the other side of the gym floor, standing with a group of his friends. And he kept looking at her. Caroline didn't realize it at first. Boys hardly ever looked at her, not the way they looked at the other girls in her class, so she was sure Kevin was actually looking at someone behind her.

But there was no one behind her. Just empty bleachers. Most of the eighth graders were on the dance floor. It was, after all, the Spring Fling. Caroline should have been dancing, too, but a slow song had just begun and she had no one to dance with. The other girls who had no one to dance with had wandered off to the cafeteria or the bathroom, but Caroline was stuck on the sidelines, paralyzed by the thought that Kevin Harris was looking at her.

Every girl in the eighth grade at St. Rita's Junior High knew who Kevin Harris was. Most of them reapplied their lip gloss when they knew they might see him. Most of them had a colossal crush on him. But none felt about him the way Caroline did, she was sure. It wasn't only his dark brown hair, which he wore as shaggy as the dress code would allow, or his eyes, a startling, perfect shade of blue-green. It wasn't that he was the tallest boy in their grade or somehow made their drab school uniform seem stylish. What Caroline liked most about him was that he was nice.

A few months earlier, her pen had run out during English class. Kevin sat one seat behind her, one row over, and noticed her panicking as their teacher kept talking about the second act of *Our Town*. He leaned over and tapped Caroline on her shoulder with a pen, and when she turned around he smiled and handed it to her. She felt her cheeks flush and whispered, "Thanks." For the rest of class, she couldn't think of anything but him.

And Caroline wasn't the kind of girl who thought about boys very much. She told herself she had more important things to do, like homework and acting class and writing in her journal every night. But it wasn't entirely true. Some of her friends had boyfriends now, and Caroline still couldn't make eye contact with a boy without blushing. She still wore braces and her curly hair was hard to control and she just wasn't like the other girls in her class.

The other girls in her class, for instance, probably wouldn't be having so much trouble breathing if Kevin Harris was looking at any one of them from across the gymnasium. The lights were dimmed, the dance floor was crowded, but Caroline was now positive that Kevin was trying to make eye contact with her. She fiddled with the charm on her necklace furiously and looked down at her feet. She thought about making a beeline for the bathroom herself, but something made her stay where she was.

When she looked back up, she almost gasped. Kevin was walking toward her. His head was down and his hands were shoved in the pockets of his jeans, but he was definitely walking in her direction, right across the gym, making his way between the dancing couples. When he was finally in front of her, Caroline thought she might not be able to hear him because her heart was thudding so loudly in her ears.

"Hey Caroline," Kevin Harris said, glancing at her, making eye contact for a split second, then looking back down at his shoes.

Caroline cleared her throat. "Hi." It was all she could manage to squeak out.

"I was wondering if you wanted to dance." He said it so quickly it sounded like one long word. Caroline's world stopped right then. She wanted to remember this moment forever. Only two other boys had ever asked her to dance to a slow song. In sixth grade, at the very first school dance she ever attended, James Driscoll came up to her during the very last song. He was best known for having gone to Space Camp that summer, and for not seeming to wear deodorant. Caroline tried to smile at him as she said her ride was there and she had to go. She waited an extra 10 minutes in the parking lot for her mother to pick her up, just so she didn't have to dance with James. She felt terrible about it—for hurting James's feelings, but also about the fact that he was the only boy who asked her to dance.

In seventh grade, at the Christmas Ball, she got a slightly better offer. This time from Doug Doyle, a boy she'd known since kindergarten. But he played JV basketball and was sort of cute. She said yes, but just as she was heading onto the dance floor with him, her friend Maggie ran up and grabbed her hand. She was in tears and needed an emergency trip to the bathroom because she'd overheard some girls making fun of the dress she was wearing and wanted some moral support. Caroline apologized to Doug six times, but he never asked her to dance again.

So she was going to enjoy this moment. This moment when Kevin Harris, who had already been nice enough to lend her a pen, asked her to dance with him. She felt a smile spread across her face as she said, "OK."

Recall how the pen incident in class made Caroline feel.

"OK," he mumbled back. He turned around and she followed him into the crowd of slow dancers. There were couples making out and doing other things the chaperones wouldn't approve of, and which usually made Caroline cringe, but she didn't care about them now. She wiped her clammy hands on her skirt, hoping no one noticed, and tried to remember exactly where she should put them— on Kevin's shoulders? Around his neck? She took a quick peek at the couple they were walking past. The girl's hands were dangerously close to the boy's butt. She would definitely not be putting her hands there!

Kevin picked a spot and turned around, staring anxiously at her face. "OK," he mumbled again. Slowly, he put his arms around her waist. A shiver ran around Caroline's neck and down her back. She didn't actually put her hands anywhere; they just wound up lingering on Kevin's shoulders. He had on a soft, long-sleeved navy blue tee shirt. She would always remember that color because for a solid minute it was the only thing she could see. She shifted from foot to foot, and somehow they moved around in a circle together. It was weird being so close to a boy, especially Kevin. She felt like he would know all her secrets somehow, because she was sure he felt her heart pounding.

She found herself wondering if she might go on her first date soon. If Kevin asked her to dance, he must be thinking about asking her out.

In the middle of her reverie, Kevin stopped moving. Caroline was confused for a moment—did the song stop? Did she miss something? But everyone else was still dancing. She took a step back and saw Kevin's face was pink and blotchy.

"I can't do this," he said.

to be continued

Read-Aloud Opportunity ▶ Reading Pairs

Directions: With your teacher's guidance, pair up with another student. Read "Last Dance" on pages 77–80 aloud to each other. One of you starts by reading the first paragraph aloud. The other reads the second paragraph. Going back and forth, read all the paragraphs. Work together to figure out the pronunciation of unfamiliar words.

After You Read

Converse

Directions: Using facts and details from the first half of the story, along with your own ideas and opinions, complete the following sentences. Then, in a class or small-group discussion organized by your teacher, discuss your ideas with classmates.

1. Caroline likes Kevin because _____

   _____

   _____

2. Caroline is the kind of person who _____

   _____

   _____

3. Caroline is uncomfortable at the dance because _____

   _____

   _____

Connect

Directions: Connect to the text by comparing details in the story to your experiences in real life. Then freewrite for three to five minutes on a separate sheet of paper. Use one of the connection prompts below to get your ideas flowing. If you prefer, you can compare details in the story to a character in a TV show, movie, or book.

> **Connection Prompts**
>
> Caroline reminds me of . . .
>
> Caroline's shyness around Kevin is similar to . . .
>
> I also . . .
>
> I never . . .
>
> This story makes me feel . . .
>
> This reminds me of a time when I . . .
>
> I can understand why Caroline . . .

Write

Directions: In "Last Dance," we learn that Caroline, the main character, likes a guy named Kevin. How do you think he feels about her? And how do you think he feels about himself? Do you think he sees himself as being as attractive and nice as Caroline thinks he is? On your own paper, write a journal entry of three to five paragraphs. Write as though you were Kevin in "Last Dance" and describe your thoughts about Caroline and about yourself. Use details from the story and your own imagination to develop ideas for the journal entry.

Strategy▶

Summarize a Story

In Chapter 3, you learned how to identify main characters, main events, conflict, and resolution in a story. Then, in the first part of this chapter, you learned to recall key story details. Now this lesson will show you how to combine these elements to create an effective story summary.

Before You Read

Opinion Poll

Directions: The following statements express ideas about characters in "Last Dance." You may or may not agree with each statement. Your teacher will read each statement aloud and ask for a show of hands. Raise your hand at the appropriate time to show that you agree or disagree with the statement.

1. Caroline should have more confidence around guys like Kevin.
2. Caroline and Kevin are too different to go out with each other.
3. Kevin is probably too shy to continue dancing with Caroline.
4. Kevin is probably going to hurt Caroline.
5. Kevin and Caroline will probably end up dating.

Set a Purpose for Reading

Directions: Think about the first half of "Last Dance." What is one thing you hope to find out when you read the second half of the story? On the following lines, write what you hope to find out.

In the second half of "Last Dance," I hope to find out _____

_____

_____

While You Read

Reading Strategy Mini-Lesson

Reading Strategy ▶ Summarize a Story

To **summarize** a story is to tell the story in a nutshell. In other words, you tell the most important details, but you don't retell every little thing that happened. This means that your version is much shorter than the original, and you use your own words. An effective summary of a ten-page story, for example, may be only one or two paragraphs long.

To write an effective summary, you must know what a summary includes and what it should *not* include. A summary does not, for example, express your opinions of the story. It does not focus only on your favorite part of the story. It is not a review or a recommendation. It is simply an overall look at a story.

Summaries include certain key elements. These important parts of a summary are listed in the following box.

> ### An effective story summary tells the
> - main characters
> - main events
> - important details
> - conflict
> - resolution

A summary that leaves out one or more of these elements may confuse or mislead readers. Ultimately, creating an effective summary is a balancing act. You must include the key information without going off track or getting too detailed.

Watch This!

The Strategy in Action

Trying to summarize an entire story off the top of your head can be overwhelming. It helps to take the story in chunks. The following table contains one chunk, or section, of "Last Dance" in the left column. On the right is an example of how your thoughts might unfold as you prepare a summary of this section.

Reading Selection	Summarize a Story
from Last Dance by Megan Brady Caroline stood at the edge of her junior high's gym floor, fiddling with the charm on her necklace. Most of the time she didn't even realize she was fiddling—it was just what she did when she was nervous. And she was very nervous tonight. Kevin Harris was on the other side of the gym floor, standing with a group of his friends. And he kept looking at her.	I'll start by identifying who this story is about. The first paragraph begins with a description of a girl named Caroline. She's nervous about something. Okay, she is nervous about a guy named Kevin. Now I'll look for some important details and try to identify what's going on. They're in the gym, so maybe they're at a

Reading Selection *continued*	Summarize a Story *continued*
Caroline didn't realize it at first. Boys hardly ever looked at her, not the way they looked at the other girls in her class, so she was sure Kevin was actually looking at someone behind her. But there was no one behind her. Just empty bleachers. Most of the eighth graders were on the dance floor. It was, after all, the Spring Fling. Caroline should have been dancing, too, but a slow song had just begun and she had no one to dance with. The other girls who had no one to dance with had wandered off to the cafeteria or the bathroom, but Caroline was stuck on the sidelines, paralyzed by the thought that Kevin Harris was looking at her.	dance. Kevin is on the "other side" of the floor, with his friends. Caroline doesn't consider herself to be the kind of girl who usually attracts boys' attention. Yes, it's a dance, a Spring Fling. The dance floor is crowded and a slow song is playing. Caroline has no one to dance with, so she could escape to the bathroom, but she stays because she's wondering what will happen with Kevin. I'll stop and summarize what I've read so far. ***Summary:*** "Last Dance" is about a girl who has a crush on a boy named Kevin. At the Spring Fling, she notices him looking at her, and she waits to see whether anything will happen.

Give It a Try

Summarize a Story

Directions: Finish reading "Last Dance," on pages 85–86. Then, on your own paper, write a summary of the full story (pages 77–80 and 85–86). Follow these helpful steps:

1. Take the story section by section.
2. Record your thoughts and a rough summary of each section. Be sure to use your own words—don't copy from the story.
3. Read what you've written. Go over the checklist of things to include and note any elements that are missing from your rough summary.
4. On fresh paper, write the final draft of the story summary.

> **Things to Include in a Summary**
>
> - main characters
> - main events
> - important details
> - conflict
> - resolution
>
> **Tip**
>
> A good length for this summary is three short paragraphs (think beginning, middle, and end of the story).

Reading Selection

Last Dance

by Megan Brady

continued from page 80

So many things flew through Caroline's head. Could he feel her sweaty palms through his shirt? Was he freaked out by how nervous she was? Could he tell she'd had pepperoni pizza for dinner? She knew she should have brought gum with her. Before she could ask him what was wrong, she noticed his friends still standing on the sidelines. They were laughing.

"I can't do this to you," Kevin said. "You're too nice."

"Can't do what?" Caroline asked, her mouth suddenly feeling like it was full of cotton balls.

Kevin was looking down again. "Those guys said they'd give me ten bucks if I asked you to dance." He jerked his head in the direction of his friends, who were still laughing.

Caroline blinked a few times. "What do you mean? Why?"

"Because they didn't think I would do it. They didn't think I would dance with someone who . . ." Kevin was talking to his shoes. His voice trailed off. And Caroline finally understood. This was a joke. *She* was the joke. The other couples around them had stopped dancing, too, and were watching the scene.

"I'm sorry," Kevin said, finally looking up. "I shouldn't have—"

Caroline's throat ached from the lump working its way up. She felt a sting behind her eyes. "I thought you were nice," she whispered. Before he could say anything else, she turned around and walked back to the edge of the gym floor, and then out the gym doors and down the hallway. She walked to the far girls' bathroom, past the science labs and past the classroom where she had English class with Kevin Harris. Tears were spilling down her face and she wanted to be alone. By the time she had shut herself in the last stall and sat down on the lid of the toilet, she was crying. Hard.

Why her? she wondered. What was so wrong with her? *Everything,* a little voice responded, from somewhere inside her head. How stupid she'd been to think a boy like Kevin would want to dance with her for real. Of course it was a joke. A bet. Something designed to make a big fool out of her. She should have just gone to the cafeteria with the other girls when the slow song started, instead of standing there like an idiot the way she did. She could've been drinking a soda and laughing right now instead of crying her eyes out.

> **Remember that it may help to summarize each part before writing the full summary.**

She grabbed a wad of toilet paper from the roll and blotted at her face. She had no idea what she would do now. There was no way she was going back into the gymnasium. And she couldn't go anywhere else with her eyes puffy and her face all red. She looked at her watch and realized there was almost an hour left until her mom would pick her up. She pulled her knees up to her chest and a new wave of tears wet her cheeks.

"I am never, ever coming to another dance," she whispered to herself. "Ever."

Read-Aloud Opportunity ▶ Chain Reading

Directions: Your teacher will appoint a reading leader. To start the activity, this leader reads aloud the first sentence in the reading selection, beginning on page 80. As soon as he or she finishes the sentence, the next person in line reads the next sentence aloud, and so on around the room. When the last person has read, the reading leader reads next, beginning the chain again. If someone has trouble reading a word, the reading leader should help by reading that word aloud for the person.

After You Read

Converse

Directions

1. *Think.* Read what you wrote in Set a Purpose for Reading on page 82. When you read the second half of "Last Dance," did the story reveal what you hoped to find out?

2. *Share.* With your teacher's guidance, form groups of three or four people. Share your response in Set a Purpose for Reading with the group. Then tell them whether the second half of the story met or did not satisfy your hopes, and why.

Connect

Directions: Create a story about a time someone had an embarrassing moment or was fooled by someone. What happened? Who was there? How did the person feel afterward? Jot down your ideas in note form. Save these notes to use in the Write activity that follows.

Write

Directions: Write a short summary of what happened to the person in your made-up scenario. In one or two paragraphs, tell

- who experienced an embarrassing moment
- what happened, including key details
- how things turned out

Reflections

Embarrassing Moments

This chapter opened with an illustration of a particularly embarrassing situation. (See page 71.) Did you notice the smaller elements from this scene scattered throughout the chapter?

What did the main and smaller illustrations tell you about embarrassing moments, and how does this relate to your own experience in such a situation?

What ideas did the short story give you about embarrassing moments?

Sibling Relationships

Being an Active Reader

If you've ever played video or board games, you know that winning does not always come easily. You must observe and strategize. You watch other players, try to predict their moves, and plan your own strategy. You might recall strategies you learned from past opponents. You might try a move that you learned from reading tips on a Web site. The one thing you can't do is relax and assume victory is yours.

The act of reading requires similar skills of observation and strategy. Just as you rarely win a game by pure luck, you rarely get meaning from a passage without working at it. Victory—in either scenario—doesn't just magically happen. This chapter explains how you can take charge of your reading experience by **making predictions** and **making connections**. Just like playing a game, reading a passage can reward you with the hard-won victory of understanding and meaning—but only if you take charge by being an active reader.

Strategy▶

Make Predictions

Before You Read

Preview the Passage

Directions: Read the title and paragraphs 1–6 of the story beginning on page 96. Then answer the following questions.

1. Who is the main character? _____

2. What is happening in paragraphs 1–6? _____

   _____

3. What pleases the main character in these paragraphs? _____

   _____

4. What worries the main character? _____

   _____

5. What do you think the character's main problem will be in the story? _____

   _____

Explore Key Nouns

Directions: The following table contains a list of nouns (persons, places, or things) from "Pluto," the story you just previewed and are about to read in full. Knowing what these things are will help you better understand the story.

1. *Explore.* With your teacher's guidance, pair up with a classmate. Divide the table in half. Take the nouns in your half of the table and find out what they are or what they mean. Use a dictionary, encyclopedia, Web site, and/or other resources approved by your teacher.

2. *Write.* In your own words, write an explanation of what each noun is. Then make a note of the source where you found the information.

3. *Share.* Share your information with your partner.

Nouns That Add Meaning to "Pluto" by Gail Carson Levine		
Person, Place, Thing, or Idea	**Explanation**	**Source of Information**
Androcles and the Lion		
Oscar (in film)		
choreography		
Episcopal Church		
Holocaust		
rabbi		
synagogue		
dress rehearsal (in theater)		

Nouns That Add Meaning to "Pluto" by Gail Carson Levine *continued*

Person, Place, Thing, or Idea	Explanation	Source of Information
blocking (from "to block out," in theater)		
cue (in theater)		
central casting (in theater)		
Pluto		
Mercury		

While You Read

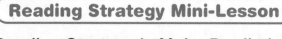

Reading Strategy Mini-Lesson

Reading Strategy ▶ Make Predictions

Have you ever found yourself in one of these situations?

Your best friend's birthday is coming up. You are walking through a store alone, looking for gift ideas. Suddenly, your eyes lock on to the perfect item. You say to yourself, "She [or he] will love this!"

You want to stay out late with your friends—later than your curfew. You think about which of your parents is more likely to let you stay out later. Then you call that parent and ask permission.

You are playing softball, and it's your turn at bat. You do a few test swings and study the outfield. The players out there are excellent catchers. If you hit the ball out there, one of them is likely to catch it, and you'd be out. So you make a decision. When the pitch comes, you bunt the ball, and it falls between you and the pitcher. You are betting that you'll make it safely to first base before the pitcher can pick up the ball and throw it to first base.

These three scenarios have something in common. In each one, you use your knowledge to **make a prediction** about what is most likely to happen next. A natural part of the reading process is making predictions.

Your first thought may be this: Making a prediction about a story means guessing the ending. Yes, this is one kind of prediction—but not the only kind. You can make predictions all throughout a story. For example, look at what you wrote in the Preview the Passage activity on page 90. After reading paragraphs 1–6 of "Pluto," you made a prediction about what Rachel's main problem would be.

Often, authors plant clues in a story to pique (grab) your curiosity and make you wonder what is going to happen next. To make a prediction, look for these clues. Then use the clues and your own knowledge and experience to guess what will happen. For example, recall the beginning of "Last Dance." Caroline is standing on the sidelines of a school dance, wondering why her crush Kevin is staring at her. A slow song is playing, and he keeps staring at her. With these clues, you can predict that he will probably ask her to dance. The story does not *tell* you that he's about to approach her, but the clues hint at it.

Making Predictions
about what will happen in a story

1. Read a short section of the story, then pause.

2. Look for details that hint at what might happen in the story.

3. Ask questions such as, "How this will turn out?" and "Will this character get what she or he wants?"

4. Use story clues, plus your own knowledge and experience, to make an educated guess about what will happen.

5. Keep reading to find out if your prediction is accurate.

As with any reader, sometimes your predictions will be right on target , and sometimes they won't be. If your prediction is off target, determine whether you missed some clues in the story, or whether you misinterpreted them. Sometimes, authors deliberately mislead readers in order to surprise or delight them later.

In any case, making predictions as you read a story helps you connect to the story, understand what is happening, and enjoy what you are reading.

Watch This!

The Strategy in Action

You have already read the first six paragraphs of "Pluto," for the Preview the Passage Activity earlier in this chapter. Now read paragraphs 7–19. Then read the example below of how you might make predictions as you read this part.

In paragraph 7, Rachel is really happy about getting the part of Lavinia. Even French class can't spoil her "happy glow." I bet that soon, her happy glow will be spoiled. This is logical because stories are about conflict, right?

In paragraph 8, Rachel says she wants to tell everyone at once. I think she is building things up so much that she will be disappointed.

Okay, paragraphs 9–12. Here's a potential source of trouble—the sister, Sara. Rachel says they fight a lot. Sara is always causing trouble. When Sara is not home on time, no one notices Rachel. I bet Sara does something to ruin Rachel's big announcement.

Next, in paragraph 13–17, Rachel's dad gets home and she's excited but won't tell him why. She is really building this up! Since her parents seem like nice, normal people, I think that they will at least congratulate her.

In paragraphs 18–19, Rachel feels like the stage is set perfectly for her big announcement. I think she will make her announcement. I predict her parents will be pleased, but Sara will somehow steal their attention away.

Give It a Try

Make Predictions

Directions: Continue reading "Pluto," picking up with paragraph 20 on page 97. As you read, notice clues that hint at conflict or actions or decisions to come. Notice when you feel suspense or curiosity. Use these moments as opportunities to make predictions. Write some of your predictions in the table on the next page.

Making Predictions about "Pluto"

Section of the Story	Your Predictions
paragraphs 20–29	
paragraphs 30–36	
paragraphs 37–42	
paragraphs 43–49	
paragraphs 50–54	
paragraphs 55–63	
paragraphs 64–66	
paragraphs 67–71	
paragraphs 72–85	

Reading Selection

Pluto

by Gail Carson Levine

1   While my heart bounced from my knees to my throat and back again, Mr. Silverberry read the list of cast members. Finally he said, "The part of Lavinia will be played by . . ."

2   It was the weirdest thing. As he began the sentence, I went into a daydream. I imagined walking to the subway with my best friend, Alicia, and explaining that I didn't get the part because I wasn't—

3   "Congratulations!"

4   Somebody poked me. Will Dietz whispered that I had the part. I hadn't heard Mr. Silverberry say ". . . played by Rachel Kahn."

5   *I actually got it!*

6   I grinned so hard my face almost split. I said, "I did? Really?" Then, out of nowhere, I flashed on telling Mom and Dad and my sister, Sara. I wondered if they'd pay attention.

7   At lunch my friends toasted me with Pepsi and Snapple and made up rave reviews and told me what to wear to the cast party. I spent the afternoon in a happy glow that even French class and Madame Miserable couldn't spoil.

8   When I got home, Mom was in the kitchen, working on dinner. I could have told her about getting the part then, but I wanted to tell everyone at once.

9   I looked for Sara. She's a senior in high school, and I'm a junior. We aren't close, maybe because we share a bedroom. *Share* isn't the right word. Our room is a demilitarized zone. We try not to escalate hostilities, and mostly we respect the rules of turf we've hammered out over the years.

10   Today she was actually home, studying in our bedroom. At least three nights a week she's late for dinner. Neither of us has to come home right after school, but we're supposed to tell Mom and Dad where we're going, and we're supposed to call if we're going to be late, and we're supposed to carry our cell phones.

11   She usually strikes out on all three. When she's very late, which is often, my parents decide that she's been mugged. They always forget that the same thing happened two nights before and she turned up perfectly healthy ten minutes after they started calling all the hospitals in New York City.

12 On those nights when they're convinced Sara is bleeding into a sewer, it wouldn't matter if I had just won an Oscar. They would be completely uninterested.

13 I took my homework into the living room. When I heard Dad unlock our apartment door, I ran to meet him.

14 "What's wrong?" he said.

15 "Nothing. Can't I greet my father without anything being wrong?" I hugged him.

16 "This is nice." He hugged me back. He smelled sweaty from the subway and cold, because it was February.

17 I followed him while he hung up his coat and went into the kitchen to hug Mom. We have a family hug routine. We hug each other and pound each other on the back at the same time. This is normal at my house, when no crisis is going on.

18 Then my father went to the bathroom, and I set the table. Sara came into the kitchen, which should have clued me in that something was up. Usually when she's home, she stays in her room till Mom has yelled twice for her and my father's face has started to turn red.

19 I felt like it was all being choreographed for me.

20 My mother ladled soup, and I carried the bowls to the table.

21 "What's new with Jack?" Dad asked. Jack Phillips is the lunatic who runs the real estate agency where Mom works.

22 Mom took a deep breath, getting ready to answer, but I jumped in first. Jack Phillips stories are never short, and I couldn't wait.

23 "I got the part of Lavinia. It's the lead in *Androcles and the Lion,* the senior play."

24 They congratulated me. Sara said it was great. Dad smiled. Mom said she was going to be a nervous wreck watching me. Would she have preferred for me *not* to get the part?

25 And then my fifteen seconds of fame were over.

26 My mother said, "I made the soup too salty."

27 Dad said, "It's delicious, Laura."

28 Mom took another deep breath to start the Jack Phillips story, but this time Sara jumped in. "I've been thinking about something." She smiled. "I want to tell you about it. It means a lot to me for you to be behind me."

Record your predictions as you read.

29 They didn't see it coming. They just waited, no foreboding on their faces. But I knew trouble was on the way. I didn't know what it was going to be, but I thought, *Look out!* I don't know who I was warning. Me, probably.

30 "You know how you always tell me I need more structure?"

31 "We've said that once or twice," Mom said, smiling.

32 "Well, I've found the way to get it. I want to be baptized. I've decided to convert to Episcopalianism."

33 My father balled up his napkin and threw it on the table. His words slammed out. "Six million did not die so you could become a Gentile." He got up and left the kitchen.

34 We're Jewish. Not religious, but Dad's parents, who both died when I was very small, were Holocaust survivors. Dad sometimes talk about how hard it was to grow up with a mother and father who'd been in a concentration camp. When he got mad at them, he couldn't act mad—behave like an ordinary kid—because of what they'd been through.

35 After Dad left the room, Mom said, "He's afraid of what he'd do if he stayed."

36 "Doesn't he want to find out why I'm doing this? Don't you?"

37 I should have told my mother about the part as soon as I got home from school. I should have taken Dad aside separately too. That would have been the way to do it.

38 "What I want to find out is how you could do this to us." Mom started clearing the soup bowls. I stood up to help, and she said "thank you" politely, as if I were a stranger.

39 My father came back in. His lips were clamped together like he'd never talk again. Mom and I brought dishes to the table, cold chicken leftovers, baked potatoes, salad.

40 I had practiced for weeks, getting ready for the audition. I hadn't told Mom and Dad or Sara about it because I wanted to surprise them. And I didn't want them to think less of me if someone else got the part.

41 Sara said, "I thought you'd be glad I've found something that's bringing meaning to my life."

42 Dad turned red, and I was scared he'd have a heart attack. Mom started humming, and Sara finally found the sense to shut up.

43 Nobody talked for a few minutes, and then I told them about getting the part, about how I was sure Melissa Jordan would get it because she was a senior and she got the lead in everything. I talked about the rehearsal schedule and about how hard memorizing my lines was going to be, because Shaw plays have such long speeches. I didn't know why I was talking. They weren't listening, even though they pretended they were. So I also found the sense to shut up, and we finished eating in silence.

44 And then I thought of something funny. *Androcles and the Lion* is about religion. It's about a bunch of early Christians who are waiting to be thrown to the lions for their beliefs.

45 If I thought Sara was anything like them—if I thought she honestly wanted to convert—I would have tried to help her. I would have stood up for her with Mom and Dad.

46 Not that she was faking. I was sure she believed she wanted to be an Episcopalian. But I was also sure that if you peeled back a dozen or so layers in my sister's crazy onion of a brain, you'd discover that what she really wanted was to stir up trouble and be the eye of my parents' cyclone.

47 It was like her lateness, only more so. When she arrives very late, after the hospital phone calls have begun, she always has a long string of explanations. Mom and Dad are always furious, and Sara always gets mad right back—because they won't sympathize with her tale of woe. It usually takes hours for the argument to simmer down and for them to forgive each other.

48 No one else ever seems to notice that Sara's explanations usually start with something avoidable—she lost her subway pass, she missed her train stop, she twisted her ankle. One story began with her getting soaked by a water fountain. A water fountain!

49 For the next few weeks home was horrible. Mom and Dad made Sara talk to the rabbi at our synagogue (which we almost never attend). They made both of us go with them to a family therapist, where Mom and Dad and Sara did all the talking. Dr. Barone never asked me how I felt about the situation, although I thought he should have. After all, I was a member of the family. Wasn't I?

50 Mom and Dad also got the name of an expert who talked kids out of being in cults. But the expert refused to talk to Sara. He said Episcopalianism wasn't a cult.

51 Meanwhile, rehearsals went well some days, not so good others. Sometimes it was lots of fun. Will, who played the lion (in a lion suit), had trouble getting his roar right, so the whole cast worked on it with him. I had a good roar. It reverberated in my chest and felt satisfying, extremely satisfying. When Will had perfected his roar, we worked with him on his purr. I liked purring, too. I liked the whole play. I pretty much memorized it, and sometimes when I was alone, I'd play all the parts.

52 Some things weren't so great, though. Mr. Silverberry kept nagging us to pick up the pace, which was hard, because Shaw plays are so wordy and the dialogue doesn't flow naturally.

53 Jason, who played Ferrovius, took forever to learn his part. Mr. Silverberry got mad at him at every rehearsal because he still had to carry his script around or get cued for almost every line. The cast was mad at him too. We might not have been fabulous actors, but at least we could memorize our lines.

54 Mr. Silverberry liked my interpretation of Lavinia, but he said I shouldn't emphasize every expression in my speeches. I should decide which were the most important and only stress them. So I tried, but I wasn't sure I was picking the right spots. I said my lines for my friend Alicia. We talked about what to accentuate, but I still wasn't certain.

55 I would have liked to ask Mom and Dad what they thought, but I didn't. I didn't exist for them these days. Oh, they were nice to me— *excruciatingly* nice—to make Sara feel how much out of favor she was by comparison. Sometimes they didn't speak to her. Sometimes they refused to let her do things she wanted to do. Sometimes they harangued her about how much she was hurting them. But when they yelled or even when they gave her the silent treatment, at least it was real.

56 So I didn't want to ask these fake nice people for help. They would only have said that I sounded good and they were sure I was remarkably talented. I might have screamed.

57 Then, about a month after her announcement, Sara told them she had changed her mind. She wasn't going to convert, but her decision had nothing to do with them. She simply wasn't certain that the Episcopal Church was the one true church. And if she had doubts, she thought it would be wrong to go through with it.

58 Mom and Dad didn't care why she changed her mind. The minute she changed it, the war was over. Everybody was happy again. The atmosphere lost its electric charge, and I stopped being scared of an explosion every time I walked into a room with Sara and my parents in it.

59 I still didn't talk about my role. I just practiced on my own and tried to make it as good as I could. Mr. Silverberry didn't criticize me again, so maybe it was better, or maybe he had given up.

60 And then the performance was a week away, and we all turned into nervous wrecks. I couldn't remember lines I could have recited backwards the week before. We mixed up the blocking. We missed our cues. Every word of our lines grew consonants, so that we couldn't pronounce anything right. We got the giggles and broke up whenever something went wrong, which was constantly.

61 Two days before the dress rehearsal, Mr. Silverberry got so upset that instead of reading his notes at the end of the rehearsal, he said, "Forget it." He put on his coat and told us to go home.

62 That made us get serious. The next rehearsal was like a dream, smooth as satin. Everybody felt good, and everybody *was* good. Backstage we kept grinning at one another.

63 That rehearsal was the first time I *felt* my part. It was especially hard to in this play, which was ninety-nine percent intellectual. But that afternoon I did it. I caught Lavinia's zeal for God, for something bigger and more important than herself. It was amazing, thrilling—to find myself thinking a made-up person's thoughts, feeling her emotions, inhabiting her. I walked on air all the way home.

64 But then dress rehearsal was a disaster. Todd, who played the captain, my romantic interest (in real life I was definitely *not* interested), had caught a cold overnight. He kept sneezing, and he couldn't pronounce the letter n. I got the hiccups in the second act, and they gave me the giggles, which everybody else caught. Jason, who had finally learned his lines, couldn't remember half of them, and Will tripped over his tail on the steps leading to the offstage arena. He completely dropped out of character and started cursing. And near the end, Mike (who played Caesar) caught his cape on a nail, and it made a ripping sound that you could have heard a mile away.

65 Then it was over. Mr. Silverberry gave us our notes. "Boys and girls," he began sweetly, "dear children, here are my notes before they cart me off to a lunatic asylum." He started listing everything that had gone wrong, and his voice got less and less sweet and more and more loud. When he was done, he didn't say we could go. He sat quietly for a minute, and then he said, "I must really be insane. I can't give up. Look. Todd, Rachel, . . ."—he named five of us who had the biggest parts—"could you stay late? Maybe we can read through the play a few more times."

66 The five of us had to check home, but we all thought we could. So Mr. Silverberry told everybody else they could leave, and he gave us a half hour to call our parents and buy stuff from the candy and soda machines.

67 On my way down to the phone in the lobby it occurred to me not to call. Just to be late. I'd be the one who showed up hours after she was expected. I'd ignore my cell phone and be the one my parents worried about. I turned around on the stairs and walked up an extra flight so I could be alone to think.

68 Mom and Dad would get scared about me sooner than they got scared about Sara because I was never late. I pictured it. Mom would be getting dinner ready. She'd wonder where I was. Dad would come home and I still wouldn't be there. Maybe Sara would be late too. I hoped she would be, because they wouldn't worry about her at all, not compared to me. They would panic. They'd call hospitals, and they'd babble about what a good child I was, how considerate, how utterly reliable. This was wonderful, like picturing my own funeral.

69 But then I had another thought, and before I even finished thinking it, I started crying. Sobbing my head off. Because I was sure they wouldn't remember I was in a play. I tried to catch my breath—I was sobbing and gasping. Sure, they would come to the performance when I reminded them. But I knew they'd forgotten I was going to be the female lead in the senior play. They had no idea that kids told me they thought I was a terrific actor, that I had worked harder on this part than I had ever worked on anything, that this was the most exciting thing that had happened to me since being born.

70 I stopped thinking and just cried. And felt terrible. And cried.

71 Finally my tears slowed down and stopped. Twenty minutes of our break had gone by. My nose was stuffed. My eyes had to be bloodshot. I stood up and headed for the bathroom so no one would see me till I washed my face.

72 If I didn't call, Mom and Dad would be frantic by the time I got home. I turned on the tap and splashed cold water into my eyes. They'd be furious, and the atmosphere would go back to explosive subzero, only it would be aimed at me, and Sara would be treated to a dose of bland politeness.

73 I didn't know how long it would last for one lateness. But I could probably stretch it out if I didn't apologize enough when I did get home. I could make things miserable for days.

74 There was a yellow water stain in the sink. I stared at it. Why did I want to be the center of a family crisis? Why did I want to be alternately yelled at and ignored? Why did I want whispered parental conferences about me? Why did I want them to watch me for clues to my behavior, as though I was a new arrival from the North Pole?

75 Why did I want the role of problem daughter? Even though Sara made trouble often, she didn't seem happy when Mom and Dad were mad at her. She wasn't enjoying herself, basking in the glare of their furious attention. I didn't enjoy it when I was ignored, but I didn't need to exchange one kind of misery for another, for a worse misery. And then I thought—and the thought astonished me—Sara wasn't a problem daughter. Not really. She was the victim of central casting for our family. Somebody had to create the crises, and she always stepped in and did it. I should be grateful, because I didn't want Sara's role. I already had a role, a better one—a real one—Lavinia in *Androcles and the Lion*, by George Bernard Shaw.

76 I combed my hair, feeling better, feeling good. Usually I'm exhausted after crying for a long time, but now I was energized. I put on fresh lipstick and left the bathroom. Since I did not want the family spotlight on me, I had to call home.

77 I preferred to be on the fringe—Pluto, not Mercury—of our family's solar system.

78 Of course it would be much better to have parents who paid attention to me, Rachel, just as I was. It would have been great to get Mom and Dad's help with my role, to feel that they were rooting for me. But it was good enough to be me, the one who had acting talent (some, anyway) and who had the lead in the school play. That was good enough all by itself.

79 I dialed. Mom answered. "Rachel? Where are you? I was getting worried."

80 "I'm still at school. I'll be home by eight thirty. We're having an extra rehearsal."

81 "Oh. What are you rehearsing?"

82 I started laughing. "It's the school play, and I have the lead."

83 "Oh. That's right. I forgot."

84 "I have to go. I'm late. Bye."

85 I headed back to the auditorium. Curtain up!

Read-Aloud Opportunity ▶ Pass the Baton

Directions: Read the ending out loud, beginning with paragraph 57. Your teacher will select someone to begin by reading paragraph 57 aloud to the class. When that person is finished, she or he should name a classmate to read the next paragraph. That person should read aloud and then name the next reader, and so on, until the end.

After You Read

Converse

Directions: With your teacher's guidance, have a class discussion about readers' predictions about "Pluto." Use the questions listed at the top of the next page as starting points for discussion.

1. Did the story end as you predicted it would? What are some clues that you used to make this prediction?

2. What is one prediction you made that turned out to be accurate? What are the clues you used to make this prediction?

3. What is one prediction you made that was off target? Why do you think that happened?

4. What section of the story made you feel the most suspense or curiosity?

5. What section of the story surprised you with an unexpected turn of events?

Connect

Directions: All kids, like Rachel in "Pluto," struggle to find their place in their household. As Rachel does, it can be amusing to imagine family members as characters from central casting. If you put certain character types together, you're bound to get certain kinds of conflict, right?

Imagine the people in your household, including yourself, as stars in a made-for-TV movie. On paper, create a mock-up of an Internet Web page that showcases the movie. On your Web page, include—

- the movie's title
- a brief description of the main conflict that the lead character (you) faces
- a brief description of each character
- a "head shot" (photo of the face) of each character (a photograph, sketch, or magazine cutout, for example)

Write

Directions: Near the end of "Pluto," in paragraph 73, Rachel comes to this conclusion:

> I preferred to be on the fringe—Pluto, not Mercury—of our family's solar system.

Do you think Rachel will be content "on the fringe" for long? Based on events in the story, what do you think Rachel's life will be like one year from now? Will she be "on the fringe"? How will she feel then about her place in her family?

Write two or three paragraphs in which you make predictions about Rachel's life one year from now. Be sure to include

- a prediction about whether Rachel will be on the fringe of her family
- a prediction about whether or not Rachel will be satisfied with her place in the family
- reasons to support your predictions (including details from the story and your own knowledge and experience)

Strategy▶

Make Connections

In the first part of this chapter, you learned to make predictions as you read a story. By using your own ideas and knowledge to help make predictions, you have already practiced **making connections** to a passage. This lesson will explain more about making connections to a passage, including *personal connections, connections to other passages,* and *connections to the larger world.* As you do so, you will continue to explore the theme of sibling relationships. This time, you'll read a poem written in free verse (a poem with no particular rhyme pattern or rhythm).

Before You Read

(Quickwrite)

Directions: Whether you have siblings or not, you are sure to have opinions about **sibling relationships**. Do all siblings fight? Do all siblings love each other? Do siblings owe each other anything? Are kids with siblings better off than only children? Do you want siblings yourself, or would you rather be an only child? How much control do parents have over sibling relationships?

On your own paper, write for five minutes about the topic of sibling relationships. You can choose to answer one or more of the questions above, or write other ideas and opinions that you have.

(Make a Connection)

Directions: The passage that you are about to read is an excerpt from "Dr. Jekyll and Sister Hyde" by Sonya Sones. The author uses this title to make a connection to the well-known novel *Dr. Jekyll and Mr. Hyde* by Robert Louis Stevenson. Write responses in the following table to make this connection.

Connect "Dr. Jekyll and Sister Hyde" and *Dr. Jekyll and Mr. Hyde*	
1. What is *Dr. Jekyll and Mr. Hyde* about? (*Hint:* Consult an encyclopedia of literature or other reference source that your teacher suggests. The term "Jekyll and Hyde" is also in the dictionary.)	

Connect "Dr. Jekyll and Sister Hyde" and *Dr. Jekyll and Mr. Hyde* (*continued*)	
2. What is the theme of this chapter, printed in bold in the Quickwrite activity on the previous page?	
3. Based on the clues from steps 1 and 2, what do you predict "Dr. Jekyll and Sister Hyde" will be about?	

While You Read

Reading Strategy Mini-Lesson

Reading Strategy ▶ Make Connections

In the Quickwrite activity on the previous page, you related your personal ideas and opinions to a stated theme, sibling relationships. In doing so, you made a **personal connection** to the theme. In the Make a Connection activity you just completed, you predicted a **connection between passages** by thinking about ideas that they share.

The reading strategy of **making connections** is the practice of connecting details in a passage to yourself, to other passages, and to the world. If you think about it, you'll see that no passage exists in a vacuum. Readers create meaning from a passage by making connections between the passage and their lives, other things that they've read, and the world around them. Authors not only expect readers to make connections like these—they count on it.

The table on the next page shows three basic types of connections that readers commonly make.

Type of Connection	Explanation	Example
Text to self	*Connect the selection to your own personal experiences.* • Compare personal experiences to story events. • Relate personal ideas or opinions to a theme in a selection. • Identify with a story character. • Form new personal opinions, ideas, or beliefs in response to a selection.	• Compare how a character handles a problem with the way you handled the same type of problem. • Imagine what it would be like to have a certain character as a friend, parent, sibling, teacher, etc. • Identify qualities in a character that you want to develop in yourself.
Text to text	*Connect the selection to other things that you have read.* • Relate a story element (character, event, setting, theme) in one selection to an element in another selection. • Compare the style of one selection to that of another selection. • Look at how two selections deal with the same theme but with different outcomes.	• Imagine what a character in one story would say to a character in another story. • Compare how two passages—one funny and one serious—deal with the same theme. • Compare sibling relationships in two different stories about siblings.
Text to world	*Connect the selection to the world you live in.* • Relate an event or idea in a selection to an event or issue in a real-life community, city, state, or country. • Compare a place or group of people in a selection to a place or group in real life.	• Imagine how students in your school would react to a story event or character. • Compare the town in a story to a real town that it reminds you of. • Ask what a work of historical fiction can reveal to you about real events, people, or ideas in that historical era.

Watch This!

The Strategy in Action

The first stanza of the excerpt from "Dr. Jekyll and Sister Hyde" is printed below. Following the stanza are examples of how your thoughts might unfold as you make connections to the poem.

Making Connections

from **Dr. Jekyll and Sister Hyde by Sonya Sones**
Living under the same roof
for fourteen long years
with the world's most evil sister.
When she isn't busy pulverizing me,
she's screaming things so hideous
that I can't even repeat them here.

Connection	Explanation
Text to self	I have a sister, too, but she isn't evil, and she doesn't "pulverize" me. In fact, she ignores me completely. It's like I don't even exist to her. I think she wishes she were an only child. Sometimes I wish she <u>would</u> fight with me, just to show she knows I'm alive.
Text to text	Hmm. What does this part of the poem remind me of? I can't think of another selection. Well, that's not true. I thought of the fairy tale "Hansel and Gretel" right away. It's about siblings—a brother and sister—who are kidnapped by an evil woman in a gingerbread house. They are smart enough to escape. That makes me think of "Cinderella," which is about conflict between stepsisters. In "Hansel and Gretel" the siblings love each other and help each other survive, but in "Cinderella"

Connection *continued*	Explanation *continued*
	the evil stepsisters hate Cinderella and treat her like a servant.
Text to world	I can't help but think of the kids out there who wish they had a brother or sister, but they don't have one. How do they feel when they read about siblings fighting? Do they think that if they had a sibling, they wouldn't fight? Do they think kids with siblings take their relationship for granted? My aunt volunteers as a Big Sister in the Big Brothers and Big Sisters program. I think her Little Sister would love to have a real sister, not just a volunteer sister, whether they fought or not. But some people love being the only child.

Make Connections

Directions: Read the poem "Dr. Jekyll and Sister Hyde" on pages 111–114. Then make connections to part of the poem by following the directions below.

Making Connections to "Dr. Jekyll and Sister Hyde"

1. Choose a specific part of the poem to work with. This part could be a character, a scene, a specific stanza, a theme, an idea, or other element. In the space below, identify or describe the part of the poem you have chosen. **Part of poem:**

2. Make connections to the part of the poem that you described in step 1. In the table on the next page, write the connections that you make.

Connection	Explanation
Text to self Connect the selection to your own personal experiences.	
Text to text Connect the selection to other things that you have read.	
Text to world Connect the selection to the world you live in.	

Reading Selection

from Dr. Jekyll and Sister Hyde[1]

by Sonya Sones

IT'S NOT EASY BEING ME

Living under the same roof
for fourteen long years
with the world's most evil sister.
When she isn't busy pulverizing me,
she's screaming things so hideous
that I can't even repeat them here.

But I *don't* want pity.
That's why I never

---

[1] The title is a play on an old novel, *Dr. Jekyll and Mr. Hyde* (1886) by Robert Louis Stevenson, about a doctor with two personalities.

complain to my friends about her.
I can't stand that
"oh, Sasha, you poor thing" stuff.
I'm lots of things, but I am *not* a *poor* thing.

Besides.
My life could be worse.
I haven't been sexually molested.
I'm not battling leukemia.
My legs haven't been blown off by a land mine.
I don't even have athlete's foot.

True.
I have to live with Lucy.
But in seven hundred and thirty-nine days
she'll be going off to college.
I can tough it out till then.
I think.

IF I FOCUS ON HER *GOOD* SIDE

Lucy *does* have a good side.
She's got a side so good that she
even volunteers at Saint John's Hospital
every Tuesday afternoon
to hold the babies born with AIDS.

And she doesn't do it
because of how it will look
on her college applications.
I can tell by the light that's in her eyes
when she comes home, afterwards.

It's the same light that's there
on Thursday nights,
after she's been out delivering
Meals-on-Wheels.
Yup. She does that, too.

And she's even nice to *me*, sometimes.
But I try to keep my guard up.

Because it can all change
in a blink.
And it usually does.

She'll do things like spend hours and hours
knitting me an amazing sweater for Christmas,
but then get mad at me
and unravel the whole thing
before I ever have a chance to wear it.

> Can you make any connections here? Do you know anyone who's like this, sibling or not?

Or she'll treat me to a movie,
and even buy me popcorn,
but then refuse to sit next to me
because she says
I'm eating it too loud.

When she's being nice,
she's so nice, nicer than nice,
that I get mesmerized into trusting her,
into thinking that she'll never be awful again—
and then she puts my headlights out.

It's like living with Dr. Jekyll and Sister Hyde.

TAKE THIS MORNING, FOR INSTANCE

Lucy's just finished
whipping me up a batch
of her killer (no pun intended)
blueberry pancakes.

She even peeled an orange for me.
and sliced it into sideways wheels,
the way she knows I like it.
And now she's sitting down
across from me in the breakfast nook,
asking me all about my new boyfriend, Peter.

How did we meet? She wants to know.
Was it a love-at-first-sight kind of thing?
Or did it just sort of creep up on me?

And she wants to know what it is about him
that I like so much.
And *exactly* how far we've gone.

And now she's telling me about *her* boyfriend,
this senior named Scott
who she's completely flipped over.
How even though they've been together for four months,
she still practically stops breathing
every time she sees him in the hall.

She tells me that she can't sleep at night because
she's so worried about what's going to happen
next year when Scott goes off to college.
And that she just hates the way
Mom's so unbelievably Dark Ages
when it comes to sex before marriage.

And sitting here with her,
sharing our secrets like this,
almost feels like sisters are supposed to feel.
Except for the fear—
hovering around the edges
of our conversation like a jittery ghost.

The fear
that somehow I'll *do* something wrong
or *say* something wrong—
and make it all disappear.

Read-Aloud Opportunity ▶ Echo Reading

Directions: In this activity, a reading leader reads aloud a line from "Dr. Jekyll and Sister Hyde," and the class echoes by reading the same line aloud. Your teacher will appoint three reading leaders—one each for "It's Not Easy Being Me," "*If* I Focus on Her *Good* Side," and "Take This Morning, for Instance."

The first reading leader begins by reading the first line aloud, then pausing. The class echoes by reading the same line aloud. The leader then reads the next line, and the class echoes, and so on to the end of that section. Then the next reading leader begins.

After You Read

Converse

Directions

1. *Converse.* With your teacher's guidance, form groups of four people. Share some of the strongest connections that you made in the Give It a Try activity on page 110. As a group, make a list of your strongest Text to Text connections and Text to World connections. Aim for three or four items in each list.

2. *Regroup.* Regroup with the entire class. Together, create a master list of connections to "Dr. Jekyll and Sister Hyde," based on the lists created by each group. Did people tend to make the same connections, or was there a wide variety of connections? Why do you think this is? Discuss whether any of the connections surprise you, pique your interest, or make you want to read other selections.

Connect

Directions

1. *Think.* Imagine a meeting between Rachel from "Pluto" and Sasha from "Dr. Jekyll and Sister Hyde." What do you think these two girls would tell each other about their older sisters? What kind of advice would they share with each other? What is most important about sibling relationships to each character?

2. *Pair.* With your teacher's guidance, pair up with another student. Use your ideas from step 1 to write a short skit about Rachel and Sasha. Include dialogue in which the girls discuss sibling relationships and offer advice to each other. Aim for a skit that is three to five minutes long.

3. *Perform.* Your teacher will organize a performance schedule to give you an opportunity to perform your skit for the class.

Write

Directions

1. *Read.* Read the first two stanzas of the excerpt from "Dr. Jekyll and Sister Hyde" again, on page 111. Notice that the two stanzas are formed from six sentences, with no particular rhyme scheme or rhythm.

2. *Write.* Write down a few of your strongest ideas, opinions, or insights about sibling relationships. Organize your thoughts into six to ten sentences.

3. *Arrange.* Arrange the sentences you wrote into one or more stanzas of poetry. Give your poem a title that expresses its main idea.

Reflections

Sibling Relationships

This chapter opened with an illustration showing two brothers playing a friendly game of basketball. (See page 89.) Did you notice the close ups from this illustration scattered throughout the chapter?

What do the boys' expressions and body language tell you about sibling relationships?

How does the situation in the illustration compare to the sibling relationships you just read about? How does it compare to your own experience with a sibling or a very close friend?

Stepping Back

Reread a Selection

Now that you've completed Chapters 1 through 5, go back and choose a favorite selection to reread. On your own paper, answer the question below.

> 1. What selection did you choose and what purpose can you set for reading it (aside from the purpose of answering this question)?

Reread the selection with your purpose in mind and then answer the questions that follow.

> 2. What did you notice about the story the second time that you didn't notice the first?
>
> 3. Did you notice anything different about your reading habits this time?
>
> 4. What is the purpose of rereading a story?

Read a New Selection

In Chapter 2, you read the beginning of the story "Harrison Bergeron." Go back and look at it (it begins on page 26) to refresh your memory. Then read the rest of the story, below. Describe your experiences on the pages that follow.

from Harrison Bergeron

by Kurt Vonnegut Jr.

continued from page 29

The television program was suddenly interrupted for a news bulletin. It wasn't clear at first as to what the bulletin was about, since the announcer, like all announcers, had a serious speech impediment. For about half a minute, and in a state of high excitement, the announcer tried to say, "Ladies and gentlemen—"

He finally gave up, handed the bulletin to a ballerina to read.

"That's all right—" Hazel said of the announcer, "he tried. That's the big thing. He tried to do the best he could with what God gave him. He should get a nice raise for trying so hard."

"Ladies and gentlemen," said the ballerina, reading the bulletin. She must have been extraordinarily beautiful, because the mask she wore was hideous. And it was easy to see that she was the strongest and most graceful of all the dancers, for her handicap bags were as big as those worn by two-hundred-pound men.

And she had to apologize at once for her voice, which was a very unfair voice for a woman to use. Her voice was a warm, luminous, timeless melody. "Excuse me—" she said, and she began again, making her voice absolutely uncompetitive.

"Harrison Bergeron, age fourteen," she said in a grackle squawk, "has just escaped from jail, where he was held on suspicion of plotting to overthrow the government. He is a genius and an athlete, is under-handicapped, and should be regarded as extremely dangerous."

A police photograph of Harrison Bergeron was flashed on the screen—upside down, then sideways, upside down again, then right side up. The picture showed the full length of Harrison against a background calibrated in feet and inches. He was exactly seven feet tall.

The rest of Harrison's appearance was Halloween and hardware. Nobody had ever worn heavier handicaps. He had outgrown hindrances faster than the H-G men could think them up. Instead of a little ear radio for a mental handicap, he wore a tremendous pair of earphones, and spectacles with thick wavy lenses. The spectacles were intended to make him not only half blind, but to give him whanging headaches besides.

Scrap metal was hung all over him. Ordinarily, there was a certain symmetry, a military neatness to the handicaps issued to strong people, but Harrison looked like a walking junkyard. In the race of life, Harrison carried three hundred pounds.

And to offset his good looks, the H-G men required that he wear at all times a red rubber ball for a nose, keep his eyebrows shaved off, and cover his even white teeth with black caps at snaggle-tooth random.

"If you see this boy," said the ballerina, "do not—I repeat, do not—try to reason with him."

There was the shriek of a door being torn from its hinges.

Screams and barking cries of consternation came from the television set. The photograph of Harrison Bergeron on the screen jumped again and again, as though dancing to the tune of an earthquake.

George Bergeron correctly identified the earthquake, and well he might have—for many was the time his own home had danced to the same crashing tune. "My God—" said George, "that must be Harrison!"

The realization was blasted from his mind instantly by the sound of an automobile collision in his head.

When George could open his eyes again, the photograph of Harrison was gone. A living, breathing Harrison filled the screen.

Clanking, clownish, and huge, Harrison stood in the center of the studio. The knob of the uprooted studio door was still in his hand. Ballerinas, technicians, musicians, and announcers cowered on their knees before him, expecting to die.

"I am the Emperor!" cried Harrison. "Do you hear? I am the Emperor! Everybody must do what I say at once!" He stamped his foot and the studio shook.

"Even as I stand here—" he bellowed, "crippled, hobbled, sickened—I am a greater ruler than any man who ever lived! Now watch me become what I *can* become!"

Harrison tore the straps of his handicap harness like wet tissue paper, tore straps guaranteed to support five thousand pounds.

Harrison's scrap-iron handicaps crashed to the floor.

Harrison thrust his thumbs under the bar of the padlock that secured his head harness. The bar snapped like celery. Harrison smashed his headphones and spectacles against the wall.

He flung away his rubber-ball nose, revealed a man that would have awed Thor, the god of thunder.

"I shall now select my Empress!" he said, looking down on the cowering people. "Let the first woman who dares rise to her feet claim her mate and her throne!"

A moment passed, and then a ballerina arose, swaying like a willow.

Harrison plucked the mental handicap from her ear, snapped off her physical handicaps with marvelous delicacy. Last of all, he removed her mask.

She was blindingly beautiful.

"Now," said Harrison, taking her hand, "shall we show the people the meaning of the word dance? Music!" he commanded.

The musicians scrambled back into their chairs, and Harrison stripped them of their handicaps, too. "Play your best," he told them, "and I'll make you barons and dukes and earls."

The music began. It was normal at first—cheap, silly, false. But Harrison snatched two musicians from their chairs, waved them like batons as he sang the music as he wanted it played. He slammed them back into their chairs.

The music began again and was much improved.

Harrison and his Empress merely listened to the music for a while—listened gravely, as though synchronizing their heartbeats with it.

They shifted their weights to their toes.

Harrison placed his big hands on the girl's tiny waist, letting her sense the weightlessness that would soon be hers.

And then, in an explosion of joy and grace, into the air they sprang!

Not only were the laws of the land abandoned, but the law of gravity and the laws of motion as well.

They reeled, whirled, swiveled, flounced, capered, gamboled, and spun.

They leaped like deer on the moon.

The studio ceiling was thirty feet high, but each leap brought the dancers nearer to it. It became their obvious intention to kiss the ceiling.

They kissed it.

And then, neutralizing gravity with love and pure will, they remained suspended in air inches below the ceiling, and they kissed each other for a long, long time.

It was then that Diana Moon Glampers, the Handicapper General, came into the studio with a double-barreled ten-gauge shotgun. She fired twice, and the Emperor and the Empress were dead before they hit the floor.

Diana Moon Glampers loaded the gun again. She aimed it at the musicians and told them they had ten seconds to get their handicaps back on.

It was then that the Bergerons' television tube burned out.

Hazel turned to comment about the blackout to George.

But George had gone out into the kitchen for a can of beer.

George came back in with the beer, paused while a handicap signal shook him up. And then he sat down again. "You been crying?" he said to Hazel.

"Yup," she said.

"What about?" he said.

"I forget," she said. "Something real sad on television."

"What was it?" he said.

"It's all kind of mixed up in my mind," said Hazel.

"Forget sad things," said George.

"I always do," said Hazel.

"That's my girl," said George. He winced. There was the sound of a riveting gun in his head.

"Gee—I could tell that one was a doozy," said Hazel.

"You can say that again," said George.

"Gee—" said Hazel, "I could tell that one was a doozy."

Describe your experience reading the rest of this story. What strategies, if any, from Chapters 1–5 did you find yourself using? Here are the strategies you have learned so far:

Set a Purpose for Reading

Monitor Your Understanding

Question the Text

Visualize What the Text Describes

Identify Main Characters and Main Events

Identify Conflict and Resolution

Recall Story Details

Summarize a Story

Make Predictions

Make Connections

Chapter 6

Choices

Making Sense Out of Order of Events

Have you ever thought about this? You can set an mp3 player to play songs in random order, but you cannot set a DVD player to play movie scenes in random order. The reason why is probably obvious to you—a movie wouldn't make sense if the events were told out of sequence.

Whether performed, spoken, or written, a story usually follows a predictable pattern. Events are presented in **chronological order**, the order in which they happen. In this chapter, you'll read "Confession," a story about a group of boys who decide to take action against local gangs. As you read, you'll practice identifying chronological order. You'll also learn about two techniques—**foreshadowing** and **flashback**—that authors use to build suspense and give insight into characters' motivations.

Strategy ▶
Identify Chronological Order

Before You Read

(Anticipation Guide)

Directions: Read each statement and decide whether you agree or disagree with it. If you agree, write YES on the line under Before Reading. If you disagree, write NO. At the end of this chapter, you will return to this page to complete the After Reading column.

Before Reading		After Reading
_____	1. The end justifies the means. In other words, only the results matter, not how you achieved something.	_____
_____	2. Whatever happens is fate.	_____
_____	3. The right choice is usually obvious.	_____
_____	4. Some people make better choices than other people.	_____
_____	5. There are no bad people, just bad choices.	_____

(Instant Words)

Directions: The following words are important to the plot in "Confession," the story you are about to read. The words are listed in the order in which they appear in the story. Read the words quietly to yourself.

1.	sister	6.	cross
2.	gun	7.	teacher
3.	fight	8.	smell
4.	match	9.	spread
5.	sell	10.	burning

Did you have trouble reading any of the words? They come from a list of 1,000 common English words, words that readers should know on sight, without sounding them out and without stumbling over them.

Use the words in the list, along with the title of the story, to make predictions about the story. What kind of problem do you think the main character faces? Where do you think some of the events take place? Write your prediction on the lines that follow, using as many words from the list as possible. *Note:* You can add prefixes or suffixes to the words to create different forms. For example, *match* can become *matches*, and *sell* can become *selling*.

_____

_____

_____

_____

While You Read

(**Reading Strategy Mini-Lesson**)

Reading Strategy ▶ Identify Chronological Order

As children, before we could read, we listened to stories that adults told us and read to us. We followed along as events unfolded. What happened next? And then what happened? And after that? How did it end? By listening, we became familiar with the way events are organized in stories. In a plot, events are generally told in the order in which they happened. This pattern is called **chronological order**.

You can identify the pattern of chronological order in all kinds of narratives. (A narrative is a piece of writing that tells a series of events.) The following table lists examples of narratives that are usually arranged in chronological order. It also lists some words that authors use to make the order of events logical and clear.

Chronological Order *The pattern of organizing events in the order in which they happened*			
Words That Signal Time Order			
first	next	then	finally
last	before	later	afterward
soon as	meanwhile	during	
Examples			
• A *short story* tells a short series of events involving one or more characters. • A *novel* tells a long series of events involving one or more characters. • A *narrative poem* tells a series of events involving one or more characters in verse form.			

Chronological Order
continued

- A *biography* tells a series of true events from a real person's life, written by someone other than that person.
- An *autobiography* tells a series of true events in the author's life.
- A *historical account* tells about one or more events in history, such as a war or journey of exploration.

Watch This!

The Strategy in Action

Read paragraphs 1–21 of "Confession," beginning on page 127. Then read the following example of how you might identify the order of events in these paragraphs.

The first paragraph is the police report. It mentions April 10 and 17, but the story doesn't really begin until the next paragraph. I think the story will either be about what led up to JJ being arrested, or what happens after the arrest.

In the second paragraph I don't see any clues to time order. The narrator is just asking questions. Nothing is happening yet.

The first sentence of paragraph 3 gives clues to the sequence of events. The words "last year" tell me that everything started last year. In the next sentence, "just after" tells me that everything started "just after" Danny's sister was raped.

Paragraphs 4–21 are about a conversation the boys have when they form the Protectors. They debate what the club should do, and they decide what their goals should be. This whole conversation seems like one event.

Here is how I can map the events of the story so far:

Timeline of Events in "Confession"

Danny's sister is raped.	Danny starts the Protectors club.
Clues/signal words:	*Clues/signal words:*
• "last year"	• "just after" Danny's sister is raped
	• "when we began seventh grade"

Give It a Try

Identify Chronological Order

Directions: Continue reading "Confession," picking up with paragraph 22 on page 129, and identifying the sequence of events. Follow these steps:

1. Circle signal words or phrases that help make the sequence of events clear (or write the words/phrases on sticky notes).

2. Draw a line across the page to mark off actions and events.

3. On your own paper, create a timeline that shows the sequence of events in "Confession." Using the example on the previous page as a model, list each action or event, along with related clues or signal words from the story.

Reading Selection

Confession
by Gloria D. Miklowitz

1 POLICE REPORT: THE FOLLOWING IS THE STATEMENT OF THE THIRTEEN-YEAR-OLD JIM JAMES, KNOWN AS JJ, IN THE SHOOTING OF SAMBOY PARKS AT FIFTH AND ELM, SAN GABRIEL, APRIL 10. JAMES AND THREE OTHER MEMBERS OF THE PROTECTORS GANG HAVE BEEN REMANDED TO JUVENILE HALL TO AWAIT HEARING ON APRIL 17.

---

2 Why'd we form the Protectors? You gotta ask? I mean, what about the graffiti? What about the gangs? What about the drugs in school and nobody cares about it? Christ, you can't go to the john without risking your life! You gotta ask?

3 Danny started the club last year when we began seventh grade. Just after his sister got raped right in their building. They never caught the guys who did it, either, though we had our suspicions. That was when I made up my mind. Nobody gonna do that to Lacey, my kid sister. Not if I could help it.

4 Danny got us together. That's me—JJ, Carlos, and Bruno. We been friends since second grade. Danny says, "What we gonna do about the hood? Stand around and let the gangs take over?"

5 "What *can* we do?" Bruno asked. "We're just four kids. They got guns. They got big numbers."

6 "Yeah," Carlos added. "They got *power*, man."

7 Danny's been itching for revenge ever since what happened to his sister. I couldn't blame him. I knew he had something in mind and if I waited, he'd come out with it. And he did. "I say we fight back. We form our own gang. But not like theirs. We be the Protectors!" he said.

8 "Cool!" Carlos agreed right off. I think he was dreaming of a fancy club jacket in red and gold, something to make him look big and important.

9 "Way to go!" Bruno added, always ready to agree with whatever Danny said.

10 "JJ?"

11 "I don't know," I said. "Yeah, we need protection, but what about the cops? That's their job."

12 "Like much good *they* do!"

13 "What'd we do? Carry chains and knives and guns? We gonna be the law?"

14 "You chicken?"

15 "No!" My face got hot when the guys glared at me like I didn't belong.

16 "So what's your problem?"

17 "Guns," I said. "I don't like them. How we gonna fight back when all the gangs use them? Besides, the hood's got enough guns without us."

18 "Did I say we'd use guns?" Danny tapped his forehead. "We gonna use the gray stuff. We gonna *persuade* and *negotiate*. That's how we gonna deal with our problems."

19 Didn't make sense to me. I thought about the kids dealing drugs at school. About the locker thieves and the risks you took going to the toilet alone. *Persuade* and *negotiate* with guys like that? Come *on*!

20 "We won't use weapons," Danny promised. "We'll use other methods. Satisfied?"

21 Bruno and Carlos waited for me to answer. "Yeah, I guess," I said, shrugging. "But no guns!"

---

22 "Where you going?" Lacey asked, running after me to the door. I'd come home from school just long enough to check that she was safe. And long enough to bag the paper and matches Danny asked us to bring.

23 "Out. And you can't come. Lock up behind me."

24 "I'm coming!" Lacey grabbed my arm and her eyes got big with hope. She spends a lot of time alone, watching TV after school. Going out's a treat. Suddenly she noticed the bag.

25 "What're you hiding?" She danced around, trying to grab the bag from behind my back. "JJ! You selling dope? I'm gonna tell!" she cried.

26 "I'm not dealing dope!"

27 "So, what's in the bag?"

28 "Nothing!"

29 "You're lying!"

30 Feeling cocky about what I was about to do and mad that she thought I could be a dealer, I said, "All *right*!" and told her about the Protectors. It was dumb because it was boasting and I knew it. If it ever got out who the Protectors were, we'd be in bad trouble. Not just with the cops, either.

31 I took Lacey by the shoulders and squinted at her real mean. "Now listen good! What I just said is a secret, hear? You can't tell a soul, not a soul!"

32 Lacey stared at me like I was God. "I wouldn't, JJ. You know I wouldn't tell!" she promised. "Cross my heart."

---

33 The first job we planned was against Rolf Steiner and his Eastside gang druggies at school. I met Danny and the guys at the back door to the gym. Bruno had a key. He didn't say how he got it.

34 We slid into the building and headed for the lockers. I could hear the band practicing in the auditorium and my heart flipped in my throat. I felt like a SWAT team guy must feel just before doing something dangerous.

35 Halfway to the lockers we heard the security guard coming. Danny motioned and we ducked into the rest room. We each took a stall and crouched on the toilet lid so our legs wouldn't show. The guard came in, whistling. I could hear him pee in the stall next to mine and jammed a hand over my mouth to hold back the giggles.

36 We'd agreed in advance on the targets—three lockers. The lockers belonged to guys in the Eastside gang you didn't mess with. They came to school mostly to do business. And their business was selling drugs. Sometimes you'd see one or another in class, sitting in back with arms folded over long-sleeved khaki shirts no matter what the weather. He'd be half-stoned and chewing gum and no one, not even the teacher, called him on it. Not since Mr. Hyde got beat up on his way home from school and not since Mrs. Ramos went to the hospital when five guys cornered her and did things she wouldn't talk about for fear of worse.

> **Note the sequence of events as you read.**

37 It made sense, going after thugs like that. We saw ourselves as vigilantes. We weren't out for blood. We just wanted to persuade the Eastsiders to move their business elsewhere. Out of our school, at least. That's how we thought.

38 Danny stood watch and each of us took a locker, one we knew belonged to a gang member. I laid my bag on the ground and drew out the paper. I slid sheets into the cracks under and around the locker so the door looked like it wore a ruffle. Down from me I saw Bruno and Carlos struggling to slide their papers in place, too. Then I pulled out the matches. I could imagine all the stuff inside the locker, the smelly sneakers and gym clothes, the battered books, candy wrappers, bags of rock cocaine, the pills, the grass. And I felt good.

39 Danny came to my side. "Ready?"

40 "Yeah!"

41 "Go!"

42 He pulled a lighter from a pocket and lit one sheet of paper, then moved to Carlos's locker, then Bruno's. "Symbolic," he said. "This way I'm responsible, too." As he went down the line I lit the rest of the pages around my locker. The white sheets crisped into dark brown smoking curls real fast and the fire spread inside. Pretty soon you could smell burning trash and chemicals.

43 "Way to go," Carlos whispered, raising a fist in triumph.

44 "Should we maybe leave a message?" Bruno asked.

45 "JJ?"

46 "No. I think we should get outta here, fast!" I said. "Don't leave anything to tie this to us." I grabbed my empty sack and tossed it.

47 "He's right, guys, let's go!" Danny said.

48 We turned around and raced down the halls to the back door. I was proud. We hadn't used weapons. Score one for *persuasion*.

to be continued

Read-Aloud Opportunity ▶ Independent Reading

Directions

1. *Read alone.* On your own, go back over the first half of "Confession," on pages 127–131. On the page or on sticky notes, mark words that stand out as more difficult to read than most words. Practice reading these words aloud.

2. *List words.* Choose ten of the words you marked in step 1. On your own paper, list them in the order in which they appear in the story.

3. *Read aloud.* With your teacher's guidance, form groups of three or four people. Read your list of words aloud to the group. Compare your list with the other lists. Did people tend to list the same words, or do the words vary from person to person? Discuss what makes a word challenging to read. Is it the number of syllables? The spelling? Whether or not it is familiar?

After You Read

Converse

Directions: As a class, discuss the choices that confront JJ in the first half of "Confession." (If necessary, go back to the timeline you made on page 127 to refresh your memory of the choices he faces.) Point out the decisions he has to make and what he chooses to do in each instance. What do these choices say about JJ's world, and about JJ himself? How do you feel about the choices he makes? Evaluate whether you think he was capable of choosing different actions and decisions than those he did choose. What choices would you make in similar circumstances?

Connect

Directions

1. *Discuss.* With your teacher's guidance, form groups of three or four people. In your group, discuss whether the events in "Confession" could happen at your school, to people you know. Why or why not? How would teachers and school leaders handle the events? How would students react? How would you react?

2. *Write.* Using ideas you developed in step 1, write an op-ed piece for your school newspaper. (An op-ed is a newspaper article that primarily expresses opinions rather than giving facts and information.) Explain whether you think your school is a safe environment and whether school officials should make any changes in safety practices. Be sure to use reasons and examples to make your opinions clear. Aim for an op-ed piece of about 200 words.

Write

Directions: Imagine that a Web site for teens is looking for stories about difficult choices young people have made. The identities of these young people will not be revealed. For the Web site, write a narrative of three to five paragraphs, telling about a difficult choice you have made. In your narrative, be sure to

- explain the situation you were in and the choice that you faced
- tell what your choice was and how things turned out
- use signal words, where possible, to make the sequence of events clear
- tell what happened in chronological order

Strategy▶
Understand Foreshadowing and Flashback

During a story, authors build suspense and heighten the reader's interest by using **foreshadowing** and **flashback**. Foreshadowing enables the author to direct the reader's attention forward, to what might happen later in the story. Foreshadowing helps readers make predictions about what might happen next. A flashback allows the author to show the reader an event that happened before the story began.

As you continue reading "Confession" and complete the activities in this part of the lesson, you'll see how foreshadowing and flashback can make a good story even better.

Before You Read

Set a Purpose for Reading

Directions: Think about what has happened so far in "Confession," on pages 127–131. Which character captures your interest the most? What would you like to find out by reading the rest of the story? On the lines below, write your purpose for reading the rest of "Confession."

My purpose for reading the rest of "Confession":

_____

_____

_____

Interpret Idioms

Directions: The author of "Confession" uses *idioms* to express ideas creatively and to capture your interest. An idiom is a word or phrase that is not meant to be taken literally. Instead, the idiom has an understood meaning within a region or culture. For example, if you say something was "a piece of cake," you mean it was easy. If you "give someone a hand," you help him.

With your teacher's guidance, pair up with a classmate. Work together to decide the meaning of each idiom in the table on the next page. Write your interpretation of each idiom in the right-hand column. These idioms are from the second half of the story that you're getting ready to read.

Idioms in "Confession" by Gloria D. Miklowitz	
Idiom	**Meaning**
" . . . whoever torched their lockers was <u>dead meat</u>."	
"The Pitbulls <u>got their kicks</u> from spray-painting walls . . ."	
"It <u>tickled me</u> to think we could maybe sic one gang on the other."	
"We <u>laid low</u> for a week . . ."	
"Give them a little of <u>their own medicine</u> . . ."	
"Now we park, <u>kill the lights</u>, and wait . . ."	
"We'll scout the place first. If it <u>checks out</u>, shouldn't take more than a few minutes . . ."	
"She watched me closely, expecting I'd <u>put her down</u>."	
"Don't <u>chicken out</u> on us . . ."	
"They <u>totaled your wheels</u>!"	

While You Read

Reading Strategy ▶ Understand Flashback and Foreshadowing

As you learned in the first half of this chapter, authors usually organize a narrative using *chronological order* of events. Sometimes, however, an author needs to include an event or conversation that occurred before the story began. In this case, the author may tell the event or conversation in a **flashback**. A flashback interrupts the sequence of current events to tell something that happened in the past.

Flashbacks enable authors to look backward in a sequence of events. To look forward in a sequence of events, authors use **foreshadowing**. Foreshadowing is the use of hints or clues to suggest events that will happen later in the story.

This table summarizes the literary terms taught in this chapter.

Literary Term	Explanation
Chronological order	the organization of events in the order in which they happened
Flashback	an event or conversation from the past that interrupts the chronological order of events
Foreshadowing	hints or clues to an event that will occur later in the story

Watch This!

The Strategy in Action

Read the following example of foreshadowing from the first half of "Confession."

Example	Explanation
In paragraphs 17–21 of "Confession," on page 128, the boys have a discussion about guns. JJ says clearly that he doesn't like them, and Danny promises that they won't use weapons. JJ agrees to participate, but says again, "But no guns!"	The heavy emphasis on "no guns" is a strong hint or foreshadowing that JJ will face a problem with guns later in the story.

Give It a Try

Understand Foreshadowing and Flashback

Directions: Read the second half of "Confession" on pages 137–142. Then fill out the following table. The left column contains excerpts from "Confession" that foreshadow how events will unfold. In the right column, describe what action, or type of action, the foreshadowing suggests to you.

Foreshadowing in "Confession"

Excerpt	What it Foreshadows
"This is going to be *so* easy!" Carlos chirped. He rubbed his hands together and his round face beamed. (paragraph 60)	
I got a tingling down my arms and legs. "No weapons, *right*?" I eyed his pocket. "If you say so," Danny smiled, innocent-like. "But it's dumb not to be prepared." (paragraphs 71–72)	
The end justifies the means, doesn't it? (paragraph 74)	
"Yeah, a gun, but I'm not gonna use it; you know that. It's not even loaded. It's just to scare them, in case we're cornered." (paragraph 88)	
Samboy laughed. "You ain't got the guts!" (paragraph 120)	

Confession

by Gloria D. Miklowitz

continued from page 131

49 It was all over school next day. Rolf and his gang put out word that whoever torched their lockers was dead meat. The cops came and asked questions. Mr. Adler, the principal, held the usual meeting in the auditorium. "I will not tolerate vandalism in this school!" he shouted. Like always.

50 "But he'll tolerate drugs," Danny whispered.

51 "Yeah," Bruno echoed.

52 "If anyone knows who's responsible for this latest crime, come forward. Your identity will be protected!" Adler said.

53 "Maybe we should start a rumor that it was the Pitbulls who did it," I whispered. The Pitbulls got their kicks from spray-painting walls, setting fires in wastebaskets. Like that. They were our next target. It tickled me to think we could maybe sic one gang on the other. Let them wipe each other out.

54 "Yeah," Danny said. But he knew I was kidding.

55 We laid low for a week, acting innocent and listening to the rumors. Drug sales were off, probably because the supply burned. Rolf and the Eastsiders were pretty desperate. (Their suppliers were pressing for payback.) They suspected every kid who looked their way. They pressured those who owed them and rumors spread.

56 For a while, I worried. What if Lacey bragged to a friend about me? And the friend told another friend and so on until it got back to Rolf? But as the week passed and nothing happened I relaxed and we started plans for our next action.

57 We decided to hit the Pitbulls. Give them a little of their own medicine so they'd know how it feels when their own property got trashed.

58 I liked the idea. We'd go after their wheels, what they valued most. In a way it was less dangerous than the locker raid.

No matches, knives, chains, or guns. The only stuff we'd need was screwdrivers and spray paint.

59 We planned it for a Saturday night. That's when the Bulls partied at one of their girls' houses. We could find out which house and do our job while they were partying, after midnight.

60 "This is going to be *so* easy!" Carlos chirped. He rubbed his hands together and his round face beamed.

61 "They'll be so smashed, they'll never know what hit them," Bruno said. "Not till they head home!"

62 "What about the cops?" I asked. "They patrol pretty heavy that part of town."

63 "Always worrying about the cops," Danny said, frowning. "Tell you what. We'll time them and do our stuff *after* they pass, okay?"

64 "Okay," I agreed.

65 Since the locker fire Lacey knew everything that was going on. "What if the Eastsiders think the Pitbulls did their lockers?" she asked when I told her our new plans. She watched me closely, expecting I'd put her down.

66 "Why would they think that?"

67 "The Pitbulls might want to take over their business?"

68 She had a point. If the Eastsiders didn't trust the Bulls, what better place to get them all than at one of their Saturday-night parties?"

69 "What about that?" I asked Danny, not admitting Lacey came up with the idea. "What if we run into the Eastsiders Saturday night?"

70 Danny thought a moment, then said, "Not to worry. We'll scout the place first. If it checks out, shouldn't take more than a few minutes and we're gone." He patted his jeans pocket like he forgot something.

What might Danny's reply foreshadow?

71 I got a tingling down my arms and legs. "No weapons, *right*?" I eyed his pocket.

72 "If you say so," Danny smiled, innocent-like. "But it's dumb not to be prepared."

73 I knew all along that Danny's plan to negotiate and persuade would mean action, not words. But as long as it didn't involve weapons, as long as no one got hurt, I could go with it. What we were doing wasn't right, sure, but we meant good. And our crimes were not bad like the things the gangs did.

74 The end justifies the means, doesn't it?

75 Saturday night I slipped out of the house after Mom and Pop were asleep. I wore a dark T-shirt and jeans. I had to go to the bathroom a half dozen times before leaving. Danny had "borrowed" his dad's Chevy, which was falling apart and as old as he was, thirteen. He was wearing an open flannel shirt, which he kept pulling down over a green T, like he was trying to hide his belly.

76 "Scared?" he asked when I climbed in. He handed me a ski mask and we drove off to pick up the guys.

77 "Yeah, I'm scared. You?"

78 "A little. Bring your paint and screwdriver?"

79 I held up the can. "Mine's red. What's yours?"

80 "Green. Merry Christmas!"

81 "Where is it?" I asked, pulling the mask over my head.

82 He nodded at the floor near my feet. "In that."

83 I pushed a paper bag with my shoe. It hardly moved. Sweat ran down my neck suddenly. "What's in it? Rocks?" I tried to sound lighthearted.

84 "The spray can and a couple *extra* things." Danny slowed at a corner and Carlos and Bruno jumped in. They started nervously babbling, both at once.

85 "*What* extra things?" I asked.

86 "Don't worry."

87 "I worry. Like what? A gun?"

88 "Yeah, a gun, but I'm not gonna use it; you know that. It's not even loaded. It's just to scare them, in case we're cornered."

89 "Stop the car. I'm getting out."

90 The talk in back stopped. "You can't quit now!" Carlos said.

91 "He's not leaving," Danny said. We were approaching the street where the party was going on. "Calm down, JJ. You know me. I just brought it to persuade."

92 "You promised," I said, voice squeaking. "You *promised*!" Cars were parked bumper-to-bumper in front of the brightly lit house. I saw shadows through the curtains in the living room, kids moving around, dancing.

93 "Now we park, kill the lights, and wait, right, Danny?" Bruno asked. "Until the squad car goes by?"

94 I opened the door ready to get out, ready to walk home the three miles, when Carlos gripped my shoulder. "Don't chicken out on us, JJ," he said. "We're in this together. We need you."

95 "I swear to God I won't use the gun!" Danny grabbed my arm. "See?" He bent and pulled the gun from the bag, opened the glove compartment, and shoved it in. "See? Satisfied? Okay?"

96 It wasn't okay. I didn't like what I'd got into but couldn't back out or I'd lose my best friends. I sat back in my seat, arms crossed over my chest, and stared out the window at the bungalow houses and garbage cans lined up for Monday pickup. I got more and more anxious with each minute. Finally, a patrol car came down the street, moving slow. It stopped in front of the party house, then drove on.

97 "Let's go!" Danny opened the driver's side door and leaped out. The rest of us followed. "We work together. I know the cars. Let's get at it!"

98 I felt a huge rush, even more than when we burned the lockers. Maybe because so much could go wrong. Someone could come out of the house and catch us. The Eastsiders could show up and figure things out. The cops could swing by sooner than we expected.

99 We worked fast, hardly talking. Every now and then I could hear music coming from the house, or loud voices. We spray-painted the motorcycles and six cars and punctured their tires. On the back of the last car I wrote, "Clean up the hood or we'll be back."

100 "Now, wasn't that easy?" Danny asked as we hurried back to his dad's car. "And we did it all peaceful. No knives, no chains, or guns, just like you wanted, JJ."

101 "Hey!" someone suddenly shouted from near the house. Two guys ran down the street toward us. "Hey! What're you guys up to?"

102 My mouth went dry and my heart nearly stopped as I yanked the car door open.

103 "Oh, man!" Carlos cried. "Samboy!"

104 Danny swung into the driver's seat. Locked his door and fumbled with the ignition key. Before he could start the car, Samboy and his gang surrounded us. One guy jumped on the roof and peered in at us through the windshield. Another pounded the door with a metal rod until the glass cracked.

105 The noise brought a lot of the kids out of the house and lights went on all over the block.

106 "Get out!" Samboy ordered, peering in at us, though he really couldn't tell who we were with the ski masks on.

107 "Hey, Samboy!" someone called. "They totaled your wheels!"

108 Samboy swung around and grabbed a crowbar from someone. "We're gonna whup you! Out!"

109 Carlos started to cry.

110 Bruno sounded like he was having an asthma attack.

111 I was so scared I nearly wet my pants. I prayed the patrol car would come by. Right now!

112 "Open up!" Samboy pounded on the car window with a fist. Then raised the crowbar like he was going to strike.

113 Danny kept trying to start the car. I gritted my teeth. If only we could get going, the guy on the roof would fall off and we'd be outta there, safe. Until school, anyway. But Danny couldn't get in gear and we kept stalling.

114 Samboy swung at the window and it cracked into a thousand pieces.

115 Danny screamed. From his waistband under his flannel shirt he pulled something dark. I froze.

116 "No!" I screamed, and tried to grab the gun away from him.

117 Danny stabbed me an elbow. "Shut up! Get the other one. In the glove compartment!"

118 "No!" I scrunched down in my seat like I could disappear. *He promised! I believed him! I should have known! I must have known!*

119 Danny rolled his window down and pointed the gun with both hands at Samboy. "Back off!" he screamed. "Back off or I'll shoot!" His hands shook and his voice went shrill.

120 Samboy laughed. "You ain't got the guts!"

121 "Danny, don't do it! Don't!" I cried, trying to grab his arm.

122 "Back off, or I'll shoot!" he screamed again, nudging me away. He made a strangled cry.

123 "I dare you!" Samboy said.

124 That's when the gun went off. I heard this awful roar. Danny sobbed. Carlos screamed. Bruno choked. Blood splattered all over me. All over my face and shirt!

> **125** And that's it. There's no more to say. That's the whole story. We didn't mean to hurt anyone, honest. We just wanted to make the hood better, safer.
>
> **126** Honest. I'm sorry.

Read-Aloud Opportunity ▶ Independent Reading

Directions

1. *Read alone.* On your own, go back over the second part of "Confession," on pages 137–142. On the page or on sticky notes, mark words that stand out as more difficult to read than most words. Practice reading these words aloud.

2. *Write sentences.* Choose five of the words that you marked in step 1. On your own paper, use each of the words in a sentence, for a total of five sentences. Underline the five words from the story.

3. *Read aloud.* With your teacher's guidance, form groups of three or four people. Read your sentences aloud to the group. Ask group members if the meaning of any of your words is unclear to them. Explain the meaning of your key words, if necessary.

After You Read

 **Converse**

Directions

1. *Think.* Return to the Anticipation Guide that you partially completed on page 124. Choose a character from "Confession" and write his or her name above the After Reading column. Imagine you are this character and complete the After Reading column as you think this character would most likely respond.

2. *Share.* With your teacher's guidance, form small groups. First, share your responses in the Before Reading column of the Anticipation Guide. Discuss whether you would change any of your responses now, after reading "Confession." Next, tell which character you chose for the After Reading column and share the responses you wrote as this character.

Connect

Directions: Choose option A or B.

A. Imagine that you are called to serve jury duty in a trial. The defendant's name is JJ. He has been brought to trial for his involvement in the shooting of Samboy, a known gang member. JJ explains what happened, and the court gives you a written copy of his explanation, called "Confession." You must decide what, if anything, to charge JJ with, and what his sentence, if any, will be. Write your decisions in a statement to read to your fellow jurors. In your statement, be sure to tell

- whether you believe JJ is guilty of all, some, or none of the crime, along with reasons for your decision
- what JJ's sentence should be, with reasons why this sentence is just

OR

B. Write your own script for a movie version of the trial. Don't forget to cast a prosecutor, defense lawyer, judge, witnesses, and jury.

Write

Directions: Authors sometimes use flashbacks to reveal why a character makes the choices he or she does in the chronological order of events. For example, in "Confession," Gloria Miklowitz could have included the information about Danny's sister as a flashback instead of directly explaining why Danny started the club in paragraph 3.

Select a character in "Confession" to work with. Then select an action or statement made by this character that interests you. Write a flashback in which you show something that happened in the past that helps explain the character's choice, action, or statement in the story. Identify where in the "Confession" your flashback would best fit. Use the guidelines box on the next page.

Writing Guidelines

1. Identify what you want to explain in the flashback. For example, do you want to explain why JJ chooses to follow Danny's plan despite his misgivings?

2. Brainstorm for reasons why this character would do or say what he or she did.

3. Decide what will happen in the flashback. Jot down an informal outline of the beginning, middle, and end of the scene. Identify the characters that will be included.

4. Write a rough draft of the scene, following the outline you made. Include action and dialogue that relate to your main idea (see step 1).

5. Write the final copy of the flashback. Identify where it would best fit in "Confession" by stating which paragraph it should follow.

Reflections

Choices

This chapter opened with an illustration depicting a social scene in which choices are being made. (See page 123.) Did you notice the smaller elements from this illustration scattered throughout the chapter?

What did the main and smaller illustrations tell you about choices? What ideas did the story give you about the topic?

How does this all relate to your own experience making decisions?

Chapter 7

Taking a Stand

Linking Ideas

News stories bring reports on people from all over the world right into our living rooms. We hear about decisions people make and actions they take, and we wonder, "Why did they do that?" Reporters try to answer that question. Reading about a person in the news, you may occasionally comment, "I know someone who is a lot like that!" You may say in disgust, "I would never do that in a million years."

When you speculate about the cause of an action, or note similarities and differences between people, you are noticing patterns. These kinds of patterns help shape stories and make them rewarding to read. This chapter explains more about ideas linked by **cause and effect**. It shows how to make **comparisons and contrasts** based on similarities and differences. As you work through the lessons, you'll read a short story about a teenage girl who takes a stand on a difficult issue.

Strategy▶

Recognize Cause and Effect

Before You Read

Generate Ideas

Directions: Use the following table to generate ideas about taking a stand.

Taking a Stand	
Explain What does it mean to "take a stand"?	
Speculate What do people hope to gain by taking a stand?	**Give a Personal Example** <u>Why</u> I felt I had to take a stand: _<u>How</u> I took a stand (what I did): _<u>What</u> happened because I took a stand:

Teen Movies

Directions: Think about a movie or TV show you've seen that shows cliques at a school. Then write a paragraph about how cliques are represented in the show. In your paragraph, consider the following questions. *Why do you think the director chose to divide the school like this? How do you feel about this sort of school environment—is it healthy or unhealthy? Do you think the movie or TV program shows a realistic portrayal of high school students? What, if anything, could be done to change the divisions at these kinds of schools?* If you can't think of a movie or show for this task, then write about how you think a movie *should* portray high school students. If you were to write a drama or comedy set at a typical high school, how would that school look?

While You Read

Reading Strategy Mini-Lesson

Reading Strategy ▶ Recognize Cause and Effect

Imagine these scenes unfolding in your mind:

Someone tells a silly joke, and you laugh.

Rain begins to fall, and a woman on the sidewalk opens an umbrella. Nearby, a man raises a newspaper to cover his head.

Thunder rumbles and lightning cracks. A dog howls. Hearing all these sounds, a child huddles under his blanket in bed.

Every day, you see causes and effects unfolding. A **cause** is the reason something happens. An **effect** is what happens; it is the result of the cause.

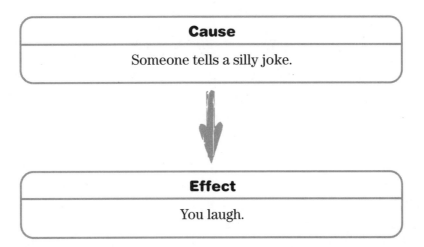

In literature, authors often use cause-and-effect patterns to organize the flow of events. You can recognize cause-and-effect relationships by asking questions and looking for clue words.

Tips for Finding Causes and Effects	
To Identify Causes • What caused the character to feel this way? • What caused the character to do this? • Why did the character make this choice?	**Words and Phrases that Signal a Cause-Effect Pattern** because as a result since so therefore consequently in response
To Identify Effects • What did the character do as a result of this emotion? • What happened as a result of this action? • What happened as a result of this choice?	

The most basic type of cause-effect relationship is one cause and one effect. This pattern is demonstrated in the example you read: *Someone tells a silly joke, and you laugh.* Note that the effect sometimes comes first: *She laughed because someone told a silly joke.* In addition, a cause-effect pattern may take other forms. You'll find a mix of cause-effect patterns in the literature that you read. The following table lists four common patterns.

Cause-and-Effect Pattern	Example
One cause and one effect	In *The Rules of Survival*, a father yells at his son, so Murdoch steps in to calm the situation.
One cause and multiple effects	In "Last Dance," Kevin asks Caroline to dance as part of a bet. As a result, she is deceived, her feelings are hurt, and she decides she doesn't want to go to any more dances.
Multiple causes and one effect	In "Cradle Hold," Harry tries to make Duke more masculine, pushes Duke to meet girls, offers unwanted advice about wrestling, and interrupts Duke's wrestling match in the county finals. As a result, Duke finally moves out of the house.

Cause-and-Effect Pattern *continued*	Example *continued*
A cause-and-effect chain	In "Confession," the Protectors get away with burning lockers. As a result, they gain confidence. Due to this confidence, they plan a more dangerous act. The danger of the plan causes Danny to take a gun. His decision to take a gun results in the shooting of Samboy.

Watch This!

The Strategy in Action

Study the following table to learn more about identifying cause and effect. First, read the paragraph from "A Letter from the Fringe." Then read the example of how your thoughts might unfold as you identify cause and effect in this paragraph.

Recognizing Cause and Effect

Reading Selection	Sample of Thought Process
from A Letter from the Fringe by Joan Bauer Gil Mishkin, whose car got covered with shaving cream last week in the parking lot. Gil doesn't have much hair because of a skin condition. His head has round, hairless patches and most of his eyebrows are gone. He can't shave and is embarrassed about it. Booker calls him "Bald Boy."	Why did Gil's car get covered with shaving cream? Here's a signal word—because. This sentence tells a cause: "a skin condition." It tells an effect: "Gil doesn't have much hair." Here are some more effects of the same cause: Gil has hairless patches on his head and basically no eyebrows. He can't shave. He is embarrassed. Booker calls him Bald Boy. All these are effects of "a skin condition." Ah, now I understand why Gil's car got covered in shaving cream. It was a prank, probably by Booker, to tease Gil about not being able to shave. The prank is also an effect of "a skin condition."

It may help you to organize your thoughts in list form. Here is an example:

<u>Cause:</u>
a skin condition
<u>Effects on Gil:</u>
—not much hair
—hairless patches on head
—almost no eyebrows
—can't shave
—embarrassment
—nickname "Bald Boy"
—prank—car covered in shaving cream

Recognize Cause and Effect

Directions: Read the first half of "A Letter from the Fringe," on pages 151–155, identifying causes and effects as you read. Use your own paper to record your findings. You may choose to use boxes and arrows to organize the causes and effects, or to use a list form.

Tips:

- Refer to the list of helpful questions and signal words on page 148.
- Authors do not always use signal words to point out causes and effects. Asking questions such as "Why?" and "What happened as a result?" is helpful when signal words are not present.
- A cause is not always stated directly. You may have to figure out a cause by reading a whole paragraph or a scene. Then state the cause in your own words.
- The effect(s) of a cause may not be stated in the same paragraph that tells the cause. Look at the scene as a whole and think about how actions are related.
- You will not find a cause or effect in every single paragraph of the story. Again, look at the scene as a whole, in addition to looking closely at individual paragraphs.

A Letter from the Fringe

by Joan Bauer

Today they got Sally.

She wasn't doing anything. Just eating a cookie her aunt had made for her. It was a serious cookie too. She'd given me one. It was still in my mouth with the white chocolate and pecans and caramel all swirling together.

I saw Doug Booker before she did.

Saw his eyes get that hard glint they always get right before he says something mean. Watched him walk toward us squeezing his hands into fists, getting psyched for the match. He's a champion varsity wrestler known for overwhelming his opponents in the first round. He was joined by Charlie Bass, brute ice hockey goalie who was smirking and laughing and looking at Sally like the mere sight of her hurt his eyes.

Get the Geeks is a popular bonding ritual among the jock flock at Bronley High.

I swallowed my cookie. Felt my stomach tense. It was too late to grab Sally and walk off.

"Fun company at four o'clock," I warned her.

Sally looked up to smirks. Her face went pale.

Booker did the vibrato thing with his voice that he thinks is so funny. "So, *Sals*, maybe you should be cutting back on those calories, huh?"

Charlie was laughing away.

"What have you got, Sals, about thirty pounds to lose? More?" He did a *tsk, tsk*. Looked her up and down with premium disgust.

All she could do was look down.

I stood up. "Get lost, Booker."

Sneer. Snort. "Now, how can I get lost in school?"

"Booker, I think you have the innate ability to get lost just about anywhere."

"Why don't you and your fat friend just get out of my face because the two of you are so butt ugly you're making me sick and I don't know if I can hold the puke in!"

He and Charlie strolled off.

There's no response to that kind of hate.

I looked at Sally, who was gripping her cookie bag.

I tried fighting through the words like my mom and dad had taught me. Taking each one apart like I'm defusing a bomb.

Was Sally fat?

I sucked in my stomach. She needed to lose some weight, but who doesn't?

Were she and I so disgusting we could make someone sick?

We're not Hollywood starlets, if that's the measuring stick.

If Booker said we were serial killers, we could have shrugged it off. But gifted bullies use partial truths. Doug knew how to march into personal territory.

I didn't know what to say. I blustered out, "They're total creeps, Sally."

No response.

"I mean, you've got a right to eat a cookie without getting hassled. You know those guys love hurting people. They think they've got some inalienable privilege—"

A tear rolled down her cheek. "I do have to lose weight, Dana."

"They don't have a right to say it!" There are all kinds of sizes in this world that are perfectly fine!"

She sat there broken, holding the cookie bag that I just noticed had pictures of balloons on it.

"It's my birthday," she said quietly.

"Oh, Sally, I didn't know that."

Sally and I were at the fringe table in the back of the lunchroom. It was as far away from the in-crowd table as you could get and still be in the cafeteria. The best thing about the fringe table is that everyone who sits at it is bonded together by strands of social victimization. We all just deal with it differently.

Present were:

Cedric Melville, arch techno whiz, hugely tall with wild-man hair and a beak nose. He has an unusual habit of standing on one leg like a flamingo. Booker calls him "Maggot."

Jewel Lardner, zany artist with pink-striped hair who has spent years studying the systems of the ICIs. ICIs are In-Crowd Individuals. She'd long ago stopped caring about being in, out, or in between.

Gil Mishkin, whose car got covered with shaving cream last week in the parking lot. Gil doesn't have much hair because of a skin condition. His head has round, hairless patches and most of his eyebrows are gone. He can't shave and is embarrassed about it. Booker calls him "Bald Boy."

> **Identify causes and effects as you read.**

"Now, with big, popular Doug," Cedric said, "you can't give him much room to move, which is what you did. When you shot right back at him, he came back harder. He always does that."

"He'll do something else, though," said Gil. "Remember what happened to my car." His hand went self-consciously over his half-bald head.

"Look," said Jewel, "you're talking defensive moves here. You've got to think offensively so the ICIs leave you alone. First off, you guys need cell phones. That way, if any of us sees big trouble coming, we can warn the others. If a jock on the prowl comes close to me, I whip out my phone and start shouting into it, 'Are you kidding me? He's got *what* kind of disease? Is it catching?' People don't come near you when you're talking about diseases."

"But most important," said Ed Looper, plunking his lunch tray down, "is you can't seem like a victim."

"I don't seem like a victim!" Sally insisted.

She did, though.

Bad posture.

Flitting eye contact.

Mumbles a lot.

I used to be that way during my freshman and sophomore years. I'd just dread having to go out in the hall to change classes. I felt like at any moment I could be bludgeoned for my sins of being too smart, not wearing expensive designer clothes, and hanging out with uncool people. I'd run in and out of the bathroom fast when the popular girls were in there.

Cedric used to skip school after being hassled. Last year he decided he'd give it back in unusual ways. Now he'll walk up to a popular group, breathe like a degenerate, and hiss, "I'm a *bibliophile*." A bibliophile is a person who loves books, but not many people know that. He'll approach a group of cheerleaders and announce, "You know, girls, I'm *bipedal* . . ." That means he has two feet, but those cheerleaders scatter like squirrels. "I'm a *thespian*," he'll say lustfully. This means he's an actor, but you know how it is with some words. If they sound bad, people don't always wait around for the vocab lesson.

Jewel also has her own unique defense mechanism. When a carload of ICIs once drove alongside her car blaring loud music, she cranked up her tape of Gregorian chants to a deafening roar. Jewel said it put a new perspective on spirituality.

People were throwing jock-avoidance suggestions at Sally, but the advice wasn't sticking.

"I just want to ignore those people," she said sadly to the group.

"Can you do it, though?" I asked her.

She shrugged, mumbled, and looked down.

See, for me, ignoring comes with its own set of problems. There are some people—Ed Looper is one of them—who can ignore the ICIs because he walks around in a cloud all day. If you want to get Looper's attention, it's best to trip him.

But *me*—sure, I can pretend I'm ignoring something or someone mean, but it doesn't help if deep down I'm steamed, and as I shove it farther and farther into the bottomless pit, the steam gets hotter.

So the biggest thing that's helped me cope is that I've stopped hoping that the mean in-crowders get punished for their cruelty. I think in some ways they have their punishment already. As my mom says, meanness never just goes out of a person—it goes back to them as well.

I look at the in-crowd table that's filling up. The beautiful Parker Cravens, Brent Fabrelli, the usual suspects. Doug Booker and Charlie Bass sit down too.

So what's inside you, Doug, that makes you so mean? If I were to put your heart under a microscope, what would I see?

Once Parker Cravens and I had to be lab partners. This was close to the worst news she'd gotten all year. She glared at me like I was a dead frog she had to dissect. Parker is stricken with *affluenza*, a condition that afflicts certain segments of the excruciatingly rich. She doesn't know or care how the other half lives; she thinks anyone who isn't wealthy is subterranean. At first I was ripped that she discounted me; then I started looking at her under the emotional microscope. I have X-ray vision from years of being ignored.

"Parker, do you like this class?" I asked.

She glanced at my non-designer sports watch that I'd gotten for two bucks at a yard sale and shuddered. "My dad's making me take it. He's a doctor and said I've got to know this dense stuff."

"What class would you rather be taking?"

She flicked a speck off her cashmere sweater, and looked at me as if my question was totally insipid.

"No, really, Parker. Which one?"

"Art history," she said.

"Why don't you take it?"

Quiet voice. "My dad won't let me."

"Why not?"

"He wants me to be a doctor."

Parker would last two nanoseconds in med school.

"That's got to be hard," I offered.

"Like granite, Dana."

It's funny. No matter how mean she gets—and Parker can get mean—every time I see her now, I don't just think she's the prettiest girl in school or the richest or the most popular; I think a little about how her father doesn't have a clue as to what she wants to be, and how much that must hurt.

to be continued

Read-Aloud Opportunity ▶ Independent Reading

Directions

1. *Read.* On your own, go back over the first part of "A Letter from the Fringe," on pages 151–155. Circle unfamiliar words (or write them on sticky notes).

2. *Share.* With your teacher's guidance, form small groups. Read aloud to your group a paragraph containing one of the words you circled in step 1. With your group members, work out the meaning of the word. If the word has a prefix, a suffix, or both, the following information may help you figure out the word's meaning.

Using Word Parts to Determine a Word's Meaning

1. Break the word into parts.

   • The main part of the word is called the *root*. This is the part to which the prefix and/or suffix is added. Examples: un**happy**, **sad**ness, re**place**able.

   • A *prefix* is added to the beginning of a root to make a new word. Examples: **mis**fire, **sub**way, **dis**agree.

   • A *suffix* is added to the end of a root to make a new word. Examples: hope**ful**, magic**al**, laugh**able**.

2. Think about the meaning of each of the word's parts. Then put the meanings together. Examples: un = "not"
   happy = "glad"
   un + happy = "not glad"

Prefixes			Suffixes		
Prefix	**Meaning**	**Example**	**Suffix**	**Meaning**	**Example**
bi-	two	bicycle	-able, -ible	able to; capable of	kissable collectible
de-	out of; opposite of; reduce	deplane dethrone degrade	-al, -ial	of; relating to; characterized by	tribal financial
dis-, dif-	not; apart; opposite of	dislike disobey diffuse	-an, -ian	of or relating to	Texan Georgian
ex-	out of; from	expose ex-wife	-ion, -tion	process condition	creation starvation
il-	not; without	illegal	-ism	a practice quality	terrorism heroism

Prefixes continued		
Prefix	**Meaning**	**Example**
im-	not	impure
in-	not	insane
re-	again; back	reheat return
sub-	under; beneath	subway
un-	not	unfair

Suffixes continued		
Suffix	**Meaning**	**Example**
-ive	tending to be a certain way	destructive
-ize	to make; to subject to	apologize sterilize
-ly	like; in such a way; every	saintly gladly daily
-ment	act of; state of being;	judgment
-ness	state or quality of being	fairness

After You Read

Converse

Directions: Participate in a class discussion about how the first half of "A Letter from the Fringe" has affected your opinions, feelings, or ideas. Point out a character whose words or actions caused a response in you. If you wish, use one of the following prompts to help express your thoughts.

Response Prompts

As a result of [specific event in the story], I have formed the opinion that . . .

What Booker said to Sally caused me to feel . . .

[Character's name] caught my attention because . . .

The conversation at the fringe table made me think of/think that . . .

The conversation between [characters' names] made me realize that . . .

A statement in the story that caused me to stop and think is . . .

Connect

Directions: What are some of the negative effects of cruelty, bullying, and peer pressure on students? What, if anything, can be done to improve a school's social environment? What can students do? What can teachers or administrators do? Freewrite for three to five minutes on this topic.

Write

Directions: With your teacher's guidance, form small groups. Review the information that each of you wrote in the Generate Ideas activity on page 146. Share your ideas for how to take a stand and discuss what methods of taking a stand seem most effective. Together, list the Top Ten Ways to Take a Stand. Write a copy of your list to post on a classroom bulletin board, wall, or other space your teacher suggests.

Strategy ▶

Make Comparisons and Contrasts

Works of literature present you with microcosms—self-contained little worlds—populated by characters in one crisis or another. One thing that makes these microcosms interesting is recognizing bits of your own real world in them—characters who remind you of your friends, your parents, your teachers, or even yourself. Reading the story allows you to see how these other people live their lives and solve their problems. **Making comparisons and contrasts** between characters and between real people and characters is one of many ways to be an active reader.

Before You Read

Investigate References

Directions: The second half of "A Letter from the Fringe" contains references to people and a book outside the story. Find out about the people and the book listed in the following table. Write a short explanation of who the person is or what the book is about.

Reference	Explanation
Albert Einstein	
Eleanor Roosevelt	
The Velveteen Rabbit	

Word Grids

Directions: Complete the word grids on the next page for the words *absurd* and *inferior.*

Step 1. Use a dictionary and thesaurus, if necessary, to complete the boxes for Definition, Synonyms, Divided into Syllables, and Antonyms.

Step 2. Use your own knowledge and ideas to list words that the key word makes you think of (in Word Association), to give an Example of the key word, to Use the Word in a Sentence, and to Sketch a simple drawing as a memory cue for the meaning of the word.

Sketch	Definition	Synonyms
	_____	_____
	_____	_____
	_____	_____
Use the Word in a Sentence		**Divided Into Syllables**
_____	**absurd**	_____
_____		_____
_____		_____
Example	**Word Association**	**Antonyms**
_____	_____	_____
_____	_____	_____
_____	_____	_____

Sketch	Definition	Synonyms
	_____	_____
	_____	_____
	_____	_____
Use the Word in a Sentence		**Divided Into Syllables**
_____	**inferior**	_____
_____		_____
_____		_____
Example	**Word Association**	**Antonyms**
_____	_____	_____
_____	_____	_____
_____	_____	_____

While You Read

Reading Strategy ▶ Make Comparisons and Contrasts

Just like real people, characters in fiction share similarities and differences with one another. For example, two best friends may share similar tastes in music and sports, but one may be outgoing while the other is painfully shy. Noticing how characters are similar and different helps you, as a reader, understand why characters behave, speak, and feel as they do. **Comparing and contrasting** characters also helps you predict events in the story and form opinions about what happens.

To make similarities or differences clear, the narrator of the story may make a direct statement. *The twins were as different as night and day. Ingrid had a ready smile and quick wit, and we all loved her. In contrast, Ivy held a grudge against the universe and had a nasty temper. We avoided her like the plague.* In direct comparisons and contrasts, signal words draw your attention to the pattern being made.

Words That Signal a Comparison or Contrast

similarly	difference	however
similar to	different from	but
likewise	in comparison	unlike
same	although	in contrast
in common	yet	by contrast
shared		

Often, similarities and differences between characters are not stated directly. You must use clues in the story, along with personal ideas and opinions, to draw conclusions about characters. Some points of similarity or difference will be more obvious than others. Some points may become clear to you only after you have read the entire story and thought about key details.

To organize clues and details that help you compare and contrast characters, you can use a Venn diagram. The next page shows an example of a Venn diagram.

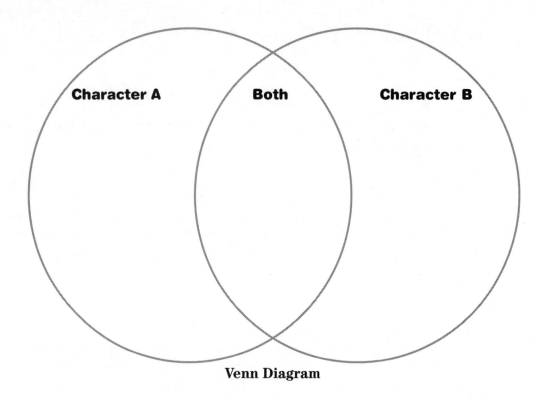

Venn Diagram

To use the diagram, list qualities that two characters share in the center, under "Both." Details that are true of only one character belong in the left or right side of the diagram, under that character's name. Completing a Venn diagram about two characters can sometimes lead you to surprising conclusions about the true nature of a character or a relationship in a story.

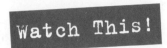

The Strategy in Action

The following Venn diagram shows how you can compare and contrast Cedric and Gil, two minor characters in "A Letter from the Fringe."

Cedric Melville

- arch techno whiz
- tall
- wild-man hair
- beak nose
- stands on one leg
- nickname "Maggot"

Both

- eats lunch at "fringe table"
- social victim
- picked on by Booker
- a friend of Dana's

Gil Mishkin

- skin condition
- bald patches
- eyebrows nearly gone
- can't shave
- nickname "Bald Boy"

Give It a Try

Make Comparisons and Contrasts

Directions: Read the second half of "A Letter from the Fringe," beginning on the next page. In the following Venn diagram, use details from the second half of the story to compare and contrast Dana and Sally.

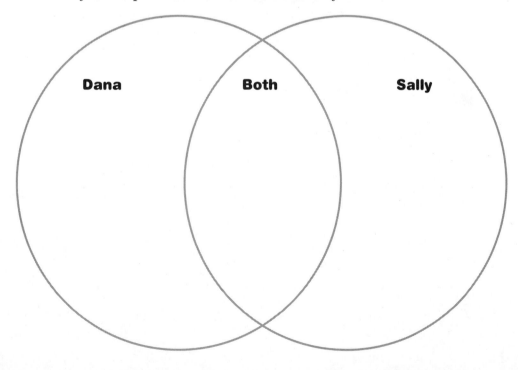

Dana   Both   Sally

Reading Selection

A Letter from the Fringe

by Joan Bauer

continued from page 155

My bedroom doesn't look like I feel. It's yellow and sunny. It's got posters of Albert Einstein and Eleanor Roosevelt and their best quotes.

Al's: *If at first the idea is not absurd, then there is no hope for it.*

Eleanor's: *No one can make you feel inferior without your consent.*

I flop on the bed wondering how come cruelty seems so easy for some people.

Wondering who decided how the boundary lines get drawn. You can never be too athletic, too popular, too gorgeous, or too rich, but you can be too smart and too nerdy.

My mom tells me sometimes people try to control others when too many things are out of control in their own lives.

I walk to my closet and pull down the Ziploc bag in which I keep my old stuffed koala bear, Qantas. He can't handle life on the bed like my other animals—he's close to falling apart. Think Velveteen Rabbit. He was a big part of my childhood. I got him when I was four and kids started giving me a hard time in nursery school because I used words that were too big for them to understand. I've talked to him ever since.

I take Qantas out of the bag, look into his scratched plastic eyes. This bear will not die.

I lost him at Disney World and found him. Lost him at the zoo and he turned up near the lion's cage. I always take him out when I've got a sticky problem. Maybe I'm remembering the power of childhood—the part that thinks a stuffed bear really holds the secrets to life.

And it's funny. As I hold him now, all kinds of things seem possible.

Like the Letter. I've been tossing the idea around all year: how could I write a letter to the ICIs. Explain what life is like from my end of the lunchroom, and maybe things would get better at my school.

At first I thought it would be easy to write. It isn't. This is as far as

I've gotten:

To my classmates at the other end of the lunchroom:

This is a difficult letter to write, but one that needs to be written.

Wrong, all wrong.

And there's the whole matter of how the letter will get distributed if I ever write it.

I could send it to the school paper.

Tack it to the front door with nails.

Print it up on my T-shirts.

I think about the mangy comments that have been hurled at me this month.

Were you born or were you hatched?

Do you have to be my lab partner?

Do you have to have your locker next to mine?

I hug my bear. Some people go on-line with their problems. I go marsupial.

"Qantas, if I had the guts to write a letter to the in crowd at my school, this is what I'd like to say:

"This letter could be from the nerd with the thick glasses in computer lab. It could be from the 'zit girl' who won't look people in the eye because she's embarrassed about her skin. It could be from the guy with the nose ring who you call queer, or any of the kids whose sizes don't balance with your ideal.

"You know, I've got things inside me—dreams and nightmares, plans and mess-ups. In that regard, we have things in common. But we never seem to connect through those common experiences because I'm so different from you.

"My being different doesn't mean that you're better than me. I think you've always assumed that I want to be like you. But I want you to know something about kids like me. We don't want to. We just want the freedom to walk down the hall without seeing your smirks, your contempt, and your looks of disgust.

"Sometimes I stand far away from you in the hall and watch what you do to other people. I wonder why you've chosen to make the world a worse place.

"I wonder, too, what really drives the whole thing. Is it hate? Is it power? Are you afraid if you get too close to me and my friends that some of our uncoolness might rub off on you? I think that what could really happen is that learning tolerance could make us happier, freer people.

"What's it going to be like when we all get older? Will we be more tolerant, or less because we haven't practiced it much? I think of the butterflies in the science museum. There are hundreds of them in cases. Hundreds of different kinds. If they were all the same, it would be so boring. You can't look at all the blue ones or the striped ones and say they shouldn't have been born. It seems like nature is trying to tell us something. Some trees are tall, some trees are short. Some places have mountains, others have deserts. Some cities are always warm, some have different seasons. Flowers are different. Animals. Why do human beings think they have the right to pick who's best—who's acceptable and who's not?

> **Compare and also contrast how Sally and Dana respond to intolerance.**

"I used to give you control over my emotions. I figured that if you said I was gross and weird, it must be true. How you choose to respond to people is up to you, but I won't let you be judge and jury. I'm going to remind you every chance I get that I have as much right to be on this earth as you."

I look at Qantas, remember bringing him to a teddy bear birthday party and being told he wasn't a real bear. I laugh about it now. He and I have never been mainstream.

I turn on my computer and begin to put it all down finally. The words just pour out, but I know the letter isn't for the ICIs and full-scale distribution.

It's for me.

And one other person.

I open my desk drawer where I keep my stash of emergency birthday cards. I pick up the one that reads: *It's your birthday. If you'd reminded me sooner, this card wouldn't be late.*

I sign the card; print the letter out, fold it in fourths so it will fit inside, and write Sally's name on the envelope.

Read-Aloud Opportunity ▶ Favorite Paragraph

Directions

1. *Select.* On your own, choose a paragraph from the second half of "A Letter from the Fringe" that speaks to you. Perhaps you agree strongly with something that Dana says or writes, or you find a statement inspiring. Practice reading this paragraph aloud.

2. *Share.* With your teacher's guidance, form groups of four students. Each person reads aloud the paragraph that he or she selected in step 1 and explains why that paragraph is noteworthy. In response, group members may make comments or ask questions about that paragraph and the reader's ideas.

After You Read

Converse

Directions: Participate in a class discussion in which you share your responses to how "A Letter from the Fringe" ended. Use one or more of the following discussion prompts to get your ideas flowing.

Discussion Prompts

- Decide whether "A Letter from the Fringe" ended the way you expected.
- Discuss whether you were satisfied with the ending.
- Did you agree with Dana's decision to give the letter to Sally and not to the In-Crowd Individuals? Why or why not?
- Why do you think Dana made this choice?
- Would you have done the same?

Connect

Directions: Use the Venn diagram on the next page to compare and contrast a character in "A Letter from the Fringe" and yourself. Choose a character you think you would be able to be friends with, despite your differences.

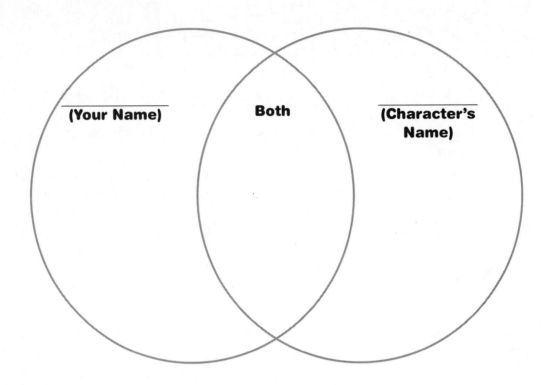

(Your Name)   Both   (Character's Name)

I would be able to be friends with _____ if this character were a real

person because _____

_____

_____

_____

_____

 **Write**

Directions

1. *Brainstorm.* With your teacher's guidance, form groups of four or five people. Together, brainstorm for a list of people who have taken a stand on a
   difficult issue. The list can include historical figures as well as people alive
   today. You can include people you know who are not public figures. The
   box on the next page lists a few ideas to get you started.

> ### People Who Have Taken a Stand on a Difficult Issue
>
> Muhammad Ali (took a stand against the Vietnam War)
>
> Rosa Parks (took a stand against racial discrimination)
>
> George Clooney (took a stand against genocide—the murder of civilians—in Darfur, Africa)
>
> Candy Lightner (founder of MADD, Mothers Against Drunk Driving, took a stand against drunk driving)
>
> Elizabeth Cady Stanton (took a stand on women's right to vote)

2. *Research.* Choose a person from your list in step 1 to write about. Research why and how this person took a stand. Find out what the person accomplished by taking a stand. If you are writing about a person whom you know personally, interview him or her to find out details and information.

3. *Write.* Write an essay of five or six paragraphs in which you

   - introduce the subject of your research and identify how this person took a stand

   - give facts and details about why and how this person took a stand

   - tell what the person accomplished by taking a stand

Reflections

Taking a Stand

This chapter opened with an illustration showing a made-up scenario in which a teen is taking a stand on something. (See page 145.) Did you notice the smaller elements from this illustration scattered throughout the chapter?

What do you think the girl might be taking a stand on, and how? How is her method different from that of the characters in "A Letter from the Fringe"?

What do you do when it comes to issues you're passionate about? Do you take a stand on them? How?

Identity

Looking Past the Surface

No one expects you to know how to play a guitar the first time you pick it up. You need to learn the basics, such as how to hold it and strum it, and how to play chords.

In the same way, a reader must start with basic skills and then build on them. At first, it is enough of a challenge to identify the main elements of a narrative, to recall key facts and details, and to summarize a work. Making predictions, connections, and comparisons requires greater skill.

In previous chapters of this book, you worked to develop these essential, invaluable skills. Now you are ready to take things a step farther. You are ready to look past the surface of a work to understand and identify unstated elements. In this chapter, you will learn to **find word meaning in context** and **identify themes**. As you work though the chapter, you'll read a short yet powerful selection with a first-person narrator who ponders his personal identity.

Strategy ▶
Find Word Meaning in Context

Before You Read

Quickwrite

Directions: Write "personal identity" at the top of a sheet of paper. Then spend five minutes jotting down your ideas about personal identity. You might answer questions such as *What does the phrase mean? Does someone's personal identity come from within that person? Or does it come from outside, from interactions with other people?* Don't worry about grammar, spelling, or punctuation—just let your ideas flow.

Literal or Figurative?

Directions: The *literal* meaning of a word is the meaning you find in a dictionary. For example, the literal meaning of *tank* is "an armored combat vehicle." Sometimes, though, we use words *figuratively* to represent an idea or image that is not the literal meaning. For example, if you call someone a *tank,* you don't mean the person is a combat vehicle. You mean that the person appears large and tough.

Think about the literal and figurative meanings of the word *invisible* in the book title *Invisible Man.* In the boxes, jot down your ideas of what "invisible man" means literally. Then write your ideas of what this phrase could mean figuratively.

invisible man (literal meaning)	invisible man (figurative meaning)

While You Read

Reading Strategy Mini-Lesson

Reading Strategy ▶ Find Word Meaning in Context

A normal part of reading is encountering unfamiliar words. Consider the word *hirsute* in the following sentence.

In my family, the men are hirsute.

An unfamiliar word can interfere with your understanding of a sentence or paragraph. If you are reading silently, you might lose your train of thought. If you are reading aloud, you might stumble, sounding out the word slowly. In either case, what you do next is important. You can

(a) shrug and go on, assuming that the word doesn't matter *or*

(b) look for **context clues**, nearby words and sentences that help you figure out the word's meaning

Choosing (a) is like encountering quicksand and thinking, "Oh, it doesn't really matter. I'll just keep walking." You get bogged down, and the whole experience is unpleasant.

Choosing (b) requires more effort on your part, but the results are worth it. You are more likely to understand the sentence, the paragraph it is in, and the passage as a whole. You become more adept as a reader and build the skills necessary to read a wide range of materials. This makes you better able to perform well in school, and it gives you an advantage outside the classroom too.

Now read the rest of the paragraph about the men who are hirsute.

I am not looking forward to becoming hirsute myself. It's one thing to have an attractive beard or a fine, thick head of hair. It's something else entirely to have shag carpet on your back. It's just embarrassing to have so much hair on your arms that your girlfriend braids it when she's bored. While many men wish they had more hair, we hirsute men wish we had less.

By continuing to read, you find clues to the meaning of *hirsute*. These clues include "shag carpet on your back," "so much hair on your arms," and the hirsute speaker wishing he had less hair. Based on these clues, you can conclude that *hirsute* means "hairy."

When you look for clues to a word's meaning in context, consider the suggestions on the next page.

Finding Word Meaning in Context

1. Read the words and phrases that make up the rest of the sentence. Ask, "Overall, what is this sentence about?"

2. Based on step 1, ask, "What word could replace the unfamiliar word in this sentence?"

3. Read nearby sentences. Look for connections to the unfamiliar word, such as comparisons, contrasts, definitions, or examples. (See the Types of Context Clues table below.)

4. Based on the clues, make an educated guess about the meaning of the word.

5. Read the sentence again, with your definition in mind. Does the sentence make sense?

Watch This!

The Strategy in Action

The following table lists different types of context clues, explains each type, and gives examples taken from stories in previous chapters of this book.

Five Types of Context Clues

Type of Clue	Explanation	Example
1. General context	Look for words, phrases, or sentences that help you make an educated guess about the meaning of the unfamiliar word.	"The picture showed the full length of Harrison against a background <u>calibrated</u> in feet and inches." (from "Harrison Bergeron" by Kurt Vonnegut Jr.) Something calibrated is marked off or divided in measurements, like a ruler.

Type of Clue continued	Explanation continued	Example continued
2. Comparison	Look for a word or phrase that is being compared to the unfamiliar word. Signal words: *also, as, in addition, like, related to, similar*	"When Duke won and the referee held his arm up in victory, Harry's face lit up brighter and brighter till it seemed ready to explode, like a star going supernova." (from "Cradle Hold" by David Klass) Exploding is like a star going supernova. A supernova must be the explosion of a star.
3. Contrast	Look for a word or phrase that is being contrasted to the unfamiliar word. Signal words: *although, but, despite, however, on the other hand, unlike*	"They just waited, no foreboding on their faces. But I knew trouble was on the way." (from "Pluto" by Gail Carson Levine) Showing "no foreboding" is contrasted to knowing that "trouble was on the way." So foreboding means "knowing that trouble is coming."
4. Example(s)	Check if examples are given that relate to the unfamiliar word. Signal words: *especially, for instance, like, such as, these, this*	"And there's the whole matter of how the letter will get distributed . . . I could send it to the school paper. Tack it to the front door with nails. Print it up on T-shirts." (from "A Letter from the Fringe" by Joan Bauer) To distribute something is to send it (like mail), to post it, or to print it for others to read.

Type of Clue *continued*	Explanation *continued*	Example *continued*
5. Definition	The context may contain a definition of the word stated directly. Signal words: *also known as, also called, in other words, that is, which are*	"Ugly faces were always <u>asymmetrical</u>; neither half looked exactly like the other." (from *Uglies* by Scott Westerfeld) <u>Asymmetrical</u> is defined right after the semicolon.

Give It a Try

Find Word Meaning in Context

Directions: The following table contains five words from *Invisible Man* by Ralph Ellison on the next page. While you read the passage, find each word and use context clues to determine the word's meaning. Then complete the table by filling in context clues from the passage and your best guess about the word's meaning. As you work, refer to Finding Word Meaning in Context (page 174) and Five Types of Context Clues (pages 174–176).

Using Context Clues to Determine Word Meaning in *Invisible Man*

Word	Context Clue(s)	Meaning
spook		
ectoplasms		
substance		
distorting		
figments		

Reading Selection

from Invisible Man

by Ralph Ellison

> **What clues help you with tough words?**

I am an invisible man. No, I am not a spook like those who haunted Edgar Allan Poe; nor am I one of your Hollywood-movie ectoplasms. I am a man of substance, of flesh and bone, fiber and liquids—and I might even be said to possess a mind. I am invisible, understand, simply because people refuse to see me. Like the bodiless heads you see sometimes in circus sideshows, it is as though I have been surrounded by mirrors of hard, distorting class. When they approach me they see only my surroundings, themselves, or figments of their imagination—indeed, everything and anything except me.

to be continued

Read-Aloud Opportunity ▶ Echo Reading

Directions: Listen as your teacher reads aloud a sentence or phrase from *Invisible Man* by Ralph Ellison. Your teacher will then pause, and the class "echoes" by reading the same sentence or phrase aloud. In this way, guided by your teacher, read the passage aloud.

After You Read

 **Converse**

Directions: With your teacher's guidance, form groups of four people. Assign each person one of the chunks of the reading selection listed in the table on the next page. Taking the chunks in order, each person reads his or her section aloud to the group and offers an explanation of what that part means. Group members may respond by asking questions and offering additional ideas. Record your group's conclusions in the Meaning column.

Section of *Invisible Man*	Meaning
I am an invisible man.	
No, I am not a spook like those who haunted Edgar Allan Poe; nor am I one of your Hollywood-movie ectoplasms. I am a man of substance, of flesh and bone, fiber and liquids— and I might even be said to possess a mind.	
I am invisible, understand, simply because people refuse to see me.	
Like the bodiless heads you see sometimes in circus sideshows, it is as though I have been surrounded by mirrors of hard, distorting glass. When they approach me they see only my surroundings, themselves, or figments of their imagination—indeed, everything and anything except me.	

Connect

Directions: Think of a time when you felt invisible to one or more people. This feeling may have lasted for a brief amount of time, or it may have lingered for a longer period of time. Why do you think you felt invisible around this person or these people? Did you want to be noticed, or did you find it desirable to be invisible at that moment? Using Ralph Ellison's paragraph as a model, write one paragraph in which you describe how it felt to be invisible and why you went unnoticed.

 **Write**

Directions: Rewrite the paragraph from *Invisible Man* as a poem in free verse. Free verse is poetry that does not have a set rhythm or rhyme pattern. The following tips will help you transform the paragraph into a poem.

1. Use Ralph Ellison's exact words. Arrange the words in lines of poetry rather than sentences in a paragraph.

2. Use each line of the poem to express a key idea, whether that idea is contained in one word or many.

3. Use line breaks to emphasize words and ideas and to set the pace of the poem.

4. Use one or more stanzas, depending on how you want to group ideas.

Strategy▶
Identify Themes

Just as you locate context clues to identify a word's meaning, you can find clues to a work's **theme**—its main message about life. Occasionally, a story directly states its theme. For example, fables by Aesop were designed to teach a moral or lesson—the theme of the tale. Traditionally, these stories end with an expression of the theme. Here are some examples:

> *Better to starve free than be a fat slave.*

> *Clothes may disguise a fool, but his words will give him away.*

> *It is easy to despise what you do not have.*

Most literary works, however, do not state a theme directly. Instead, the author uses story elements to suggest a theme that readers can identify and personalize based on their own interpretation of story elements. This section of the chapter shows you how to find clues to a story's message and put them together to identify a theme.

Before You Read

(**Theme Song**)

Directions: Many couples have a song that they refer to as "our song." It holds special meaning and symbolizes their relationship. Similarly, television shows usually have a theme song—or theme music—that expresses the main ideas or emotions associated with the show. If you could choose a theme song for your life as it is right now, what would that song be? Write your ideas on the lines below.

1. The theme song for my life right now is _____

   _____

2. I chose this song because _____

   _____

   _____

   _____

Map Ideas

Directions: If a person feels invisible wherever he or she goes, what emotions do you think that person feels? What actions would that person feel like doing? Use the main idea bubble to create an idea map about emotional and physical reactions to feeling invisible. Two ideas have been added to get you started.

Emotional and Physical Reactions to Feeling Invisible

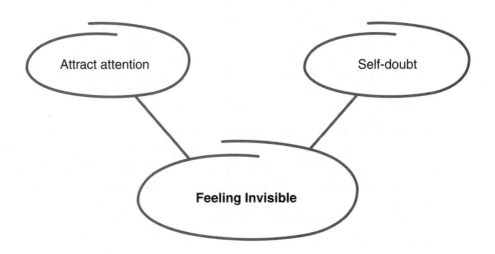

While You Read

Reading Strategy ▶ Identify Themes

Read these text messages exchanged between classmates.

> surf2000: u there?
> dollface: what's up?
> surf2000: u do the reading?
> dollface: yes
> surf2000: what you think?
> dollface: huh?
> surf2000: WHAT DID IT MEAN?
> dollface: oh. Happiness is simply a point of view.
> surf2000: u r amazing

Like surf2000, many of us read a work of literature and wonder, "What does this story mean?" or "What is this poem's message?" or "What is the author trying to tell me?" What we are working to identify is the work's **theme** or **themes**. The theme is the message or statement about life, society, or humanity that the author is trying to express. In the text message, dollface identifies a theme as "Happiness is simply a point of view."

Themes vary widely among literary works. However, you'll notice that some themes are especially meaningful to readers and recur in many works of literature. Each work brings a fresh point of view or interpretation of the theme. You may already be familiar with some of the following themes.

True love is not easy love.
Blood is thicker than water.
A person can be his [or her] own worst enemy.
Beauty is only skin deep.
Fear is stronger than love.
Love is stronger than fear.
Good fences make good neighbors.
Still waters run deep.
Where there's a will, there's a way.
Time is a great healer.

Normally, an author does not state the theme directly. Instead, the author explores the theme through the characters and plot of a story or the words and images in a poem. Using ideas and details in the literature, the reader can interpret the theme and express it in his or her own words. Asking the following questions will help you gather the details and information needed to identify a theme in a selection.

Questions to Help Identify a Theme in a Work of Literature

- What do the title, chapter titles, and any illustrations suggest about a theme?
- What does the main character's struggle or conflict tell me about a theme?
- What idea or message appears repeatedly in the selection?
- What statement or idea do I consider to be the most important in this selection?
- If the main character could express a theme to me, what would he or she say?
- What message do I take away from this selection?
- Based on my answers to the previous questions, what do I believe is a theme of the work?

Watch This!

The Strategy in Action

Think back to "A Letter from the Fringe," which you read in Chapter 7. Then study the following example of how your thoughts might unfold as you identify the theme.

Identifying Theme in "A Letter from the Fringe"

Question	Sample Response
What do the title, chapter titles, and any illustrations suggest about a theme?	The key word in the story's title is <u>fringe</u>. Dana and her friends are different from the popular crowd.
What does the main character's struggle or conflict tell me about a theme?	Dana's main problem is figuring out how to deal with mean kids like Booker. How can she make things better for herself, Sally, and the others? The issue is what to do about being different from the popular crowd.

Question *continued*	Sample Response *continued*
What idea or message appears repeatedly in the selection?	the idea of being different, being imperfect, feeling inferior
What statement or idea do I consider to be the most important in this selection?	Near the end of the story, Dana writes in her letter, "How you choose to respond to people is up to you, but I won't let you be my judge and jury. I'm going to remind you every chance I get that I have as much right to be on this earth as you." To me, that is the most important idea in the story.
If the main character could express a theme to me, what would he or she say?	Dana would say, "Everyone has a right to be who he or she is without being judged or ridiculed for it."
What message do I take away from this selection?	No one is perfect. We all have a right to be who we are without being judged.
Based on my answers to the previous questions, what do I believe is a theme of the work?	We all have a right to be who we are without being judged.

Give It a Try

Identify Theme

Directions: Read the second paragraph excerpted from *Invisible Man,* on the next page. (You may wish to go back and reread the first paragraph on page 177.) Then fill in the following table to identify a theme in this work.

Identifying Theme in *Invisible Man*

Question	Response
What do the title, chapter titles, and any illustrations suggest about a theme?	
What does the main character's struggle or conflict tell me about a theme?	
What idea or message appears repeatedly in the selection?	
What statement or idea do I consider to be the most important in this selection?	
If the main character could express a theme to me, what would he or she say?	
What message do I take away from this selection?	
Based on my answers to the previous questions, what do I believe is a theme of the work?	

Reading Selection

from Invisible Man
by Ralph Ellison

continued from page 177

Nor is my invisibility exactly a matter of a biochemical accident to my epidermis. That invisibility to which I refer occurs because of a peculiar disposition of the eyes of those with whom I come in contact. A matter of the construction of their *inner* eyes, those eyes with which they look through their physical eyes upon reality. I am not complaining, nor am I protesting either. It is sometimes advantageous to be unseen, although it is most often rather wearing on the nerves. Then too, you're constantly being bumped against by those of poor vision. Or again, you often doubt if you really exist. You wonder whether you aren't simply a phantom in other people's minds. Say, a figure in a nightmare which the sleeper tries with all his strength to destroy. It's when you feel like this that, out of resentment, you begin to bump people back. And, let me confess, you feel that way most of the time. You ache with the need to convince yourself that you do exist in the real world, that you're a part of all the sound and anguish, and you strike out with your fists, you curse and you swear to make them recognize you. And, alas, it's seldom successful.

> **What might be a theme of this text?**

Read-Aloud Opportunity ▶ Reading Pairs

Directions: With your teacher's guidance, pair up with another student. Read aloud the excerpt from *Invisible Man* on pages 184–185. Take turns reading aloud, one sentence at a time. Circle unfamiliar words, or jot them on sticky notes. Together, use context clues to figure out the meanings of these words.

After You Read

 **Converse**

Directions: Participate in a class discussion about theme in *Invisible Man.* Share what you identified as the theme. Find out how other people expressed the theme. Are your ideas similar or different? If there are differences, what do you think caused those differences? Do you think a work of literature has only one theme, or can it have multiple themes? Explain your point of view.

 **Connect**

Directions: Create a poster expressing the theme that you identified in *Invisible Man.* Use magazine cutouts, your own artwork, photographs, or other materials to create the poster. Choose to reveal the theme either through images alone, or use a combination of images and words. Your teacher will arrange an opportunity to display your work to the class.

 **Write**

Directions: The narrator in *Invisible Man* begins with the sentence, "I am an invisible man." Write two paragraphs in which you take the opposite approach. Begin with the statement, "I am a visible man [or woman]." Then discuss the things about yourself that you are proud of and that make you a person of consequence in this world.

Reflections

Identity

This chapter opened with an illustration showing someone looking at himself in the mirror. (See page 171.) Did you notice the close-ups from this illustration scattered throughout the chapter?

What did the main and smaller illustrations tell you about identity? What ideas did the readings give you about the topic?

How does this relate to your feelings about your own identity?

Chapter 9

Loss

Using Reasoning

Have you ever heard someone use the expression "reading between the lines"?

> *When Brandon wrote me after he moved away, he described new friends and activities. However, reading between the lines, I could tell he missed me and our old activities.*

> *Emma wrote a poem about the sweetness of spring, but reading between the lines, I could tell she was being sarcastic.*

By reading between the lines, you gain an added dimension of meaning from a passage. This chapter shows you how to read between the lines of a story by **making inferences** and **drawing conclusions**, and by **identifying tone and mood**. You'll read two stories narrated by characters whose words mean much more than just what's on the surface.

Strategy▶
Make Inferences and Draw Conclusions

Before You Read

Anticipation Guide

Directions: Read each statement and decide whether you agree or disagree with it. If you agree, write YES on the line under Before Reading. If you disagree, write NO. Later in the lesson, you will return to this page to complete the After Reading column.

Before Reading | | **After Reading**

_____ 1. It's hard to make friends in school. _____

_____ 2. It's important to have a lot in common with your friends. _____

_____ 3. Teens judge each other based on physical appearances. _____

_____ 4. You shouldn't have to try to impress your friends. _____

_____ 5. Friendships are the key to happiness. _____

Preview the Passage

Directions: Turn to the short story "Kerri and Me" on page 192. Examine the title and the first few sentences of the story. Based on this preview, predict what the story will be about, and set a purpose for reading it. Write your answers below.

1. What I think the story will be about: _____

    _____

    _____

2. What I hope to find out by reading the story: _____

    _____

    _____

While You Read

(**Reading Strategy Mini-Lesson**)

Reading Strategy ▶ Make Inferences and Draw Conclusions

Imagine that you get up for school one morning and look out your window. The sky is filled with low-hanging gray clouds, and you hear a rumble of thunder. From the evidence you see and hear, you can **infer** that rain will fall soon.

> An **inference** is an opinion or observation based on (1) stated or visual evidence and (2) personal knowledge.

Based on the same evidence (gray clouds and thunder), you can **conclude** that you should take an umbrella with you to school.

> A **conclusion** is a reasoned judgment based on (1) stated or visual evidence and (2) personal knowledge.

Some people do not distinguish between an inference and a conclusion. However, it is helpful to think of a conclusion as a type of inference. (A prediction, explained in Chapter 5, is another type of inference.)

You make inferences all the time. Consider these examples.

- While driving through an unfamiliar town, you see bars on all the shop windows. You infer that there is a lot of crime here.

- You go to the library to get a book that you heard about, and all the copies are checked out. You infer that the book is popular.

- You go over to your friend's house, and the driveway is empty and all the curtains are drawn. You infer that no one is home.

Look at the explanation of these examples on the next page.

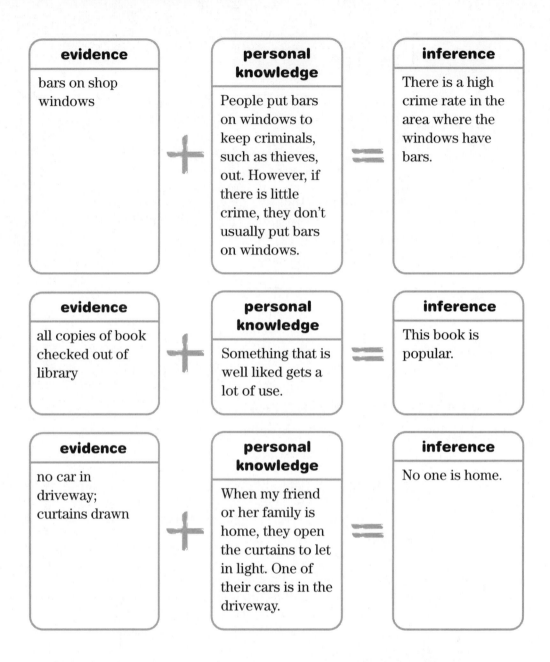

The key to making an inference is to use not only the evidence (stated details) before you but also your own knowledge. Each example above uses visible evidence *plus* personal knowledge to make the inference.

Watch This!

The Strategy in Action

On the next page is an excerpt from "Kerri and Me." Below the excerpt is an example of how you might make inferences about it.

Making Inferences and Drawing Conclusions

from **Kerri and Me by K. Ulrich**

The first time I met Kerri, I was desperate for a new friend. I had spent the entire summer dieting and riding my bike up and down hills, and I was really hoping that it would pay off—that my new looks would get me some attention, and that ninth grade would finally be the year I'd fit in.

Stated Details	Personal Knowledge	Inference/ Conclusion
The narrator doesn't say what she looks like, but she talks about "dieting," riding her "bike up and down hills," and her "new looks."	Sometimes I exercise more when I am trying to lose weight. I especially worry about what I look like right before starting a new school year.	I conclude that the narrator must have been overweight. She must not have gotten much attention in the past, and she thinks that being thinner will make her popular.
The narrator uses the words "desperate," "really hoping," and "finally."	I sometimes exaggerate and use the word "desperate" even when the situation isn't *that* urgent, but it sounds like she really does need a friend.	I can infer that the narrator didn't have any friends in school before and felt really lonely.

Give It a Try

Make Inferences and Draw Conclusions

Directions: Take a couple sheets of paper and draw lines to make three columns on each page. Label the columns *Stated Details*, *Personal Knowledge*, and *Inference/Conclusion*. Read the story "Kerri and Me," on pages 192–195. As you read, look for details that suggest more meaning than what is stated directly. Record details and your own related knowledge in the first two columns of the table. Then write your inference or conclusion in the third column.

Tip: Inferences may be large or small. You can look at sentences or at an individual word or phrase (such as "really hoping"). The goal is to understand not only what the narrator is saying but also what she is suggesting or implying.

Reading Selection

Kerri and Me

by K. Ulrich

The first time I met Kerri, I was desperate for a new friend. I had spent the entire summer dieting and riding my bike up and down hills, and I was really hoping that it would pay off—that my new looks would get me some attention, and that ninth grade would finally be the year I'd fit in.

I was never good at making friends. In middle school, everyone always seemed to have a best friend but me. I tried to crack little jokes and get in on things, but people always seemed to brush me off or give me lame excuses for not wanting to hang out. It's like they thought being overweight was contagious or something. So I spent a lot of my time by myself. Which was usually fine, seriously it was—I'm pretty good at getting by on my own. At lunch, I'd hang out in the newspaper office so I wouldn't have to deal with the cafeteria scene. But sometimes, I felt really lonely. Like when my stupid mom nagged me about the most ridiculous things, and I was SO aggravated, and I had no one to vent to. Or when something good happened, like when my article on the school election made the front page, and the editor-in-chief told me he was impressed by my reporting! I wished I had someone to share it with.

I was determined for high school to be different.

Kerri was in my freshman Earth Science class. Her smile was big and bright and her arms and legs were loose like rubber bands. Whenever she made a mistake in class she laughed loudly, not caring about the snobby kids who gawked. The problem was, Kerri already had a group of friends. *She obviously doesn't need me,* I thought. So when she turned around during one of Mr. Royal's boring lectures to whisper that I should come to her birthday, I was shocked. At first, it took a moment for her invitation to register, and then I nodded and mouthed back "sure." I tried not to seem too eager, but I was really excited.

The week before Kerri's party, I couldn't think of anything else. I couldn't wait, but I was also very nervous. Still kind of shy after all those years of being the "fat girl" at school, I had a hard time imagining that anyone would want to hang out with me. *Would people talk to me?* The night of the party, I spent forever trying on outfits. I had a lot of new clothes—thank God my mom agreed to take me shopping for back-to-school stuff—but I wasn't sure if I could pull them off. I used to wear baggy sweatpants to hide my body, but now, even though I looked much better, I wasn't sure I had the confidence for tighter things. I finally settled on a pair of dark, fitted, but not hip-hugging jeans, and I tried to make my long, frizzy hair straight and sleek. *Please don't let tonight be a disaster.*

But the party turned out to be awesome.

I could tell right away that my friendship with Kerri was meant to be. She was the first one to text prank messages to random guys from school, and when she sprayed a can of whipped cream all over her head, I laughed so hard I cried. The other girls sat in the corner rolling their eyes. But I loved how Kerri was silly, goofing around like I did at home, where no one else could see.

After the party, Kerri and I started hanging out a lot. Her mom was always out with her boyfriend and her dad lived far away, so her empty house became the perfect place to hang out after school. Soon we were doing everything together—biking in the park, studying for tests, and following boys down the hall at school. Sometimes, she would walk the long way to fourth period with me, just so that I could go by Adam Kowolski's locker and see if maybe I had the courage to talk to him. Around her, I always felt happy and more confident. We

What can you infer about their friendship?

even talked about eventually applying to the same college, maybe somewhere exciting like New York, far away from our boring small town. We planned how we'd decorate our dorm room, what we'd major in, and what fun things we'd do in the city.

When the bad news came we didn't expect it. That evening we were at her house cooking spaghetti and throwing it against the kitchen wall. It was the only way to tell when the pasta was done! When a few pieces stuck we put the rest in a bowl with sauce and carried it upstairs to Kerri's room. She had this huge walk-in closet, where we always hung out. If her mom came home she'd have to knock extra loud for us to answer, which made us feel independent and far away, like we were already living without our parents in our own dorm room. It was a pretty normal night of trying on outfits, listening to music, and thinking up new excuses to talk to Adam.

Soon after I got home from Kerri's, my cell rang.

I saw that it was her calling, but when I said hi, she didn't respond.

"Kerri? Kerri, I can't hear you." I heard muffled sobs. "Kerri, what's wrong?" What could've happened in the few hours since I'd left? "Kerri? Talk to me!"

"It's my mom," she blurted.

"Is she okay?"

"We're moving!"

I gulped. *My best friend? Moving away??* "Where?"

Before she could answer, I was crying too. What about the party next week, or the rest of high school, or our plans to go to college together? My dad opened my door and poked his head inside the room. I waved him away.

"I don't even know . . . somewhere in the Middle East!" She sobbed louder now. "How could she do this to me?"

"The what?" Our social studies teacher loved foreign affairs. She was always giving us quizzes on current events and world leaders. I knew the Middle East was far away. "Why?"

"Her stupid boyfriend. He's being transferred and she's making us go along . . ."

United Arab Emirates. The city Dubai. Deserts and camels. Hot, empty, endless sand. I'd have to google it.

I was crushed. I finally had a best friend, and now she was being taken from me. *Why is life so unfair?* I thought. *Why can't things stay good, the way they are?* My mind started racing and I saw flashbacks of myself in middle school, hunched over my lunch tray, alone in the newspaper office. Was I going to be all by myself again? In high school too?

"Are you there?" Kerri asked weakly.

I debated whether or not to share my thoughts, but decided I didn't want to seem selfish, like I was worrying about myself when she was the one moving to a completely foreign country. I had to pretend to be strong for her.

"I'm sure it won't be that bad," I tried. "I'll e-mail you every day."

Toward the end of that phone call, we decided to buy notebooks, fill them up with letters to each other, and exchange them before we left. If we read one page a day, it'd be almost like hanging out.

Though it felt like dying, this losing my best friend, it had to be worse for Kerri who was leaving everything behind. I thought about this every day I wrote. I counted down the time we had together, like they were my last days on Earth.

The day we exchanged books, we sat in her closet listening to Rihanna.

"This is the last time we're going to be here like this," I said. And then it dawned on me, what the word *last* really meant. We both started to cry. We'd already had so many last moments together—our last day in Earth Science together, our last spaghetti dinner, our last time stalking Adam down the hall.

I took her hand and squeezed it tight. She was my life support. What would happen to me once she left? Memories of my old fat self flashed through my mind and I squeezed her hand so tight she screamed.

How could I ever let her go?

My father drove me to the airport that day so I could send her off. I didn't speak the entire car ride down. I was afraid that saying anything would only make me cry. My father drove as I watched the gray sky above that would soon take Kerri away.

At the airport, her mother looked happy, which only made me mad. She'd always been so insensitive. Off in her own bubble, without thinking about what her daughter was going through.

Kerri and I tried to tune her out. We took a bunch of pictures. In all of them our faces are red and covered with sticky tears.

When it was time for them to go, I watched from afar as she and her mom walked through security. My dad put his hand on my shoulder, but I shrugged him away. Kerri was gone. In less than an hour, her plane would vanish into the sky, and I would be alone again.

Read-Aloud Opportunity ▶ Reading Circle

Directions: With your teacher's guidance, form small groups. In your group, read aloud "Kerri and Me," on pages 192–195. Follow this pattern: *First,* someone begins by reading the first sentence aloud. This person may stop with one sentence or read several sentences before stopping. *Next,* the person next in the circle picks up where the first person left off, reading one or more sentences and stopping at will. The next person picks up there and reads aloud, and so on. Continue around the circle as many times as needed to read the story aloud.

After You Read

Converse

Directions

1. *Review.* Look over the table of inferences and conclusions that you created in the Give It a Try activity on page 191. Draw a star by one or more inferences that were crucial to helping you understand the story.

2. *Share.* Share with the class an example of how you made an inference or drew a conclusion, and how that deepened your understanding of the story. Listen as other people share their inferences. Notice whether most people focused on the same parts of the story, or whether people drew conclusions from many parts of the story. Take notes about clues and inferences that did not occur to you. Think about how you will approach a story differently in the future, based on what you've learned.

Connect

Directions: In "Kerri and Me," the narrator expresses the following:

> I was never good at making friends. In middle school, everyone always seemed to have a best friend but me. I tried to crack little jokes and get in on things, but people always seemed to brush me off or give me lame excuses for not wanting to hang out. It's like they thought being overweight was contagious or something.

At one time or another, most of us feel misunderstood or wrongly judged. What do you think people assume—or infer—about you when they look at you?

What is a truth about you that they are missing—a truth which, if only they knew it, would help them draw different conclusions? On the lines below, complete the sentences to tell what people assume about you, what they should know about you, and how their assumptions would change if they knew this truth.

1. Some people look at me and see _____

_____

_____

2. If only they knew _____

_____

_____

3. Then they would _____

_____

_____

 **Write**

Directions

1. *Review.* Go back to the Anticipation Guide that you partially completed on page 188. Now imagine you are the narrator. Write "narrator" above the After Reading column. Imagine you are her and complete the After Reading column as you think she would most likely respond.

2. *Imagine.* Imagine talking with the narrator about statements in the Anticipation Guide. Do you agree or disagree with each other about each statement? If you had a conversation with the character, would it be an exploration of shared ideas? Would it be a heated argument? Would one of you work hard to persuade the other to change his or her mind about a statement?

3. *Write.* Use your ideas from step 2 to write a one- or two-page conversation between yourself and the narrator. To organize the conversation, use the format of a play, like this:

> (Your name): Write your comment here.
>
> (Narrator): Write the narrator's response and comments here.
>
> (Your name): Write your response and comments here.
> *and so on*

Strategy ▶

Identify Tone and Mood

In a work of literature, the author's word choices and the theme help to set the **tone** and **mood** of the selection. For example, if you are rushed for time, you might jot a quick note to your mom.

Gone to library, be back at dinner, love, me.

Simple words and a direct message set a casual, breezy tone. The reader, your mom, is likely to nod matter-of-factly and go on with her day. The mood is relaxed.

On the other hand, you could write a note with the same message but with a very different tone.

Due to unforeseen schedule conflicts, I am forced to confine myself to the library for the remainder of the afternoon. Afterward, I look forward to joining the family for dinner. Lovingly, your son.

This note sets a formal, even arrogant tone. Given the circumstances, the reader is likely to laugh. In spite of the formal tone, the mood is humorous.

Just as you can draw conclusions about unstated ideas in a story, you can draw conclusions about a story's tone and mood. This portion of the chapter explores tone and mood in greater depth.

Before You Read

(Journal Entry)

Directions: Sometimes you think you know someone—who he is, what he's like, why he's your friend. But then something—big or small—happens that makes you realize you didn't *really* know that person. Maybe you thought a certain girl cared only about herself, and then you saw her volunteering at a home for disabled people—and she suddenly seemed more likable. Think of a time when this kind of realization happened to you. On your own paper, write three paragraphs telling

- what you thought this person was like
- what happened to change your view of the person, and how that made you feel
- what you think about the person now

Preview the Passage

Directions: Read the title and first two paragraphs of "Through a Window" on page 203. Then jot down your reactions to the parts of the passage listed in this table. Your teacher may ask you to share your ideas with your classmates.

Part of the Story	Your Thoughts or Expectations of the Story, Based on This Part
Title	
First two paragraphs	
Words or ideas that stand out	

While You Read

Reading Strategy Mini-Lesson

Reading Strategy ▶ Identify Tone and Mood

Think about how movies begin. As the opening credits roll, music plays, and you see various shots of the characters or setting. The kind of music playing and the first glimpses of the setting get you ready for the movie. If you see a park with flowers, and the music is cheerful, you are put in the mood for a romantic comedy. If the music is creepy, and you see photos of police investigations, you are put in the mood for a thriller. The opening sets the emotional style, or **tone**, of the film. The movie produces a **mood**, or feeling, in the audience.

Like movies, literary works have tones and moods. The following table provides tips and examples on identifying tone and mood when you read.

Tone and Mood in Literature	

Tone
 	
 Tone is the emotional style of the work of literature. For example, the tone may be witty, bitter, playful, sarcastic, or spooky.
 	
 To identify tone in literature:
 Ask, "What is the emotional attitude or style of the work overall?"
 	
 Tip: If a story has more than one tone, choose the one that best describes the story as a whole. For example, if most scenes are lighthearted, but one or two scenes are sorrowful, the tone would best be described as lighthearted. However, if the tone is a mix of two emotions, then say so.
 	
 Examples:
 The tone of "Harrison Bergeron" is tongue-in-cheek, or ironic. The characters suffer painful "handicaps" but aren't fazed by it.
    The tone of "Pluto" is one of discontent. Rachel describes what it is like to live in the shadow of her older, troublesome sister.
	Mood
	
	 Mood is the feeling that a work of literature produces in the reader. For example, the mood may be happiness, peacefulness, outrage, amusement, or horror.
	
	 To identify mood in literature:
	 Ask, "What is the main emotional response that readers have to this work?"
	
	 Tip: A story may cause many different emotional responses in readers. When identifying the mood of a story, identify the most representative emotional response. As with tone, if the mood is a mix of two emotions, then describe it as such.
	
	 Examples:
	 The mood of "Harrison Bergeron" is horror. Readers feel horror at the cruelty the characters suffer at the hands of the government.
	    The mood of "Pluto" is one of sympathy. Readers like Rachel and feel that she deserves more recognition within her family.

Watch This!

The Strategy in Action

In Chapter 8, you read excerpts from *Invisible Man* by Ralph Ellison. Study the following example of how your thoughts might unfold as you identify the tone and mood in this literary work.

Identifying Tone and Mood in *Invisible Man*

Tone

First off, I notice the speaker seems serious and calm—not angry or funny, happy or sad. So one possible tone is <u>serious</u>. Or <u>somber</u>. Also, the third sentence uses the word "your," as if he is speaking directly to the reader. In the second sentence, he begins by saying "No, I am not a spook," almost like he is carrying on a conversation with the reader. So another possible tone is <u>conversational</u>. The speaker uses a lot of big words and gives a lot of examples. He seems <u>smart</u> and <u>thoughtful</u>.

I like "thoughtful" to describe the tone, but I want the word to be more specific. I looked up "thoughtful" in a thesaurus, and it listed synonyms as "contemplative," "pensive," "meditative," and "introspective." Mostly, the speaker is sharing thoughts about himself, so the best word to describe tone is <u>introspective</u>.

Mood

Now I will think about the mood of the selection. What the speaker says gets my attention. I am curious about why he feels invisible. I feel sympathy for him. I am amazed that he could seem so interesting and yet go unnoticed by other people. Since he doesn't whine and moan, I like him. I know how he feels. What word sums up my reactions in general? Hmm. Overall, from a reader's point of view, the speaker is a sympathetic character. So I will say the mood is <u>sympathetic</u>.

Give It a Try

Identify Tone and Mood

Directions: Identify tone and mood as you read "Through a Window" on pages 203–207. Use the following table to organize your thoughts.

**Identifying Tone and Mood in
"Through a Window"**

Prompts	Responses
Tone What is the emotional attitude or style of the work overall? Jot some notes and then choose the best word to describe it.	*My thoughts:* ***The tone of "Through a Window" is*** _____.
Mood What is the main emotional response that readers have to this work? Jot some notes and then choose the best word to describe it.	*My thoughts:* ***The mood of "Through a Window" is*** _____.

Through a Window

by Angela Johnson

I don't believe in God. Not right now. Not at this minute. But . . .

When they cut Nick Gorden down from the upper stairwell outside the chem lab, a storm had just come over the lake. You know the kind: lightning, rain, and wind that rips the roofs off buildings.

Ohio isn't Tornado Alley, but it comes pretty damn close. I hate it here in the spring and summer. I've just always wanted to be somewhere that nature couldn't rip my head off, and always said so. That used to make Nick laugh, 'cause he said you couldn't hide from weather—it was everywhere.

They were gentle when they took Nick away. The paramedics put him on the stretcher like he was a baby. I didn't see the rest, the cops and all. I only watched through a second-floor window as they took my best friend away from me and here and this place—forever . . .

Nick's favorite song was an old Sly & the Family Stone tune called "Everybody Is a Star." He sang it all the time. Wrote and tagged buildings everywhere with it, but in the end he didn't believe it, I guess.

It was the song Nick's uncle was singing right before he died in Vietnam. Nick's mom got all her brother's belongings—clothes, records, dog tags—from one of the guys in his platoon. That was better than some stranger showing up handing her stuff.

Nick played his uncle's records.

No CD or even cassettes ever came into the house (Nick and his mom seemed satisfied with their records). So Nick used to go to Spin-More downtown to find 45s and albums.

It used to drive me crazy listening to those old records with scratches and jumps in them, but Nick said the scratches were in his head—he knew every one of them and they were like old friends. CDs were cold and if one messed up, you couldn't put a penny on the arm of a CD to weight it down so that it wouldn't jump.

I never told Nick those records bothered me. Now I wish I had, 'cause at least it would have been one more conversation we had had.

You never understand some things until the end. Hindsight. Some things you may never understand at all.

I used to be envious of Nick, 'cause he was the person that everybody said hello to in the halls. He always smiled and seemed to sail along halls that had nothing but fear in them (to me, at least). In class pictures he always smiled. In his family pictures he always smiled.

I overheard his mom on the phone once call him sweet and good-natured.

But I found out something about Nick a week before he died that got me all turned around, and I'd known Nick since first grade. We had been each other's one and only friend since he'd followed me under the monkey bars after I'd stolen Josh Neil's lunch (Josh had hit me with an eraser earlier).

Nick had crawled under and sat with me until I gave him a Fruit Roll-Up to go away. He ate it, kept staring, and stayed.

The next day the same thing, only this time I'd taken pudding out of Heather Longchamp's backpack 'cause she'd sat on me in front of the whole first grade. Plus she always had butterscotch.

We finally got caught a week later. My mom dragged me out of the office mumbling that I was already a criminal.

Nick told the principal *he'd* taken the lunches and I said *I'd* taken them. I couldn't go out and play for two weeks. Nick's mom bought him butterscotch pudding for his lunch.

Okay, we were tight; so why didn't I understand that even though Nick was somebody that people smiled at and waved to, nobody knew anything about him? Sometimes they couldn't even remember his name. Nick said it. He was the invisible man.

The week before they took him out on a stretcher with his face covered, Mr. Miles (in civics class) couldn't remember his name or that he had even been in the class. I think Nick could have taken that if Heather (no longer eating pudding—a definite anorexic) hadn't started laughing that he'd been going to school for years and nobody ever knew his name.

I wanted to hit her. Break those skinny, skinny cheerleader arms and that big-toothed smile she only used to torture people.

Everybody laughed but me and Mr. Miles, who just looked confused and a little sorry he opened his mouth. Nick was even laughing.

I spent the rest of the day with a stomachache, not able to look Nick in the eye. Later that night he laughed that invisible people had to have a sense of humor. I didn't think that was funny.

I wasn't invisible myself. I was just visible enough to be left out of conversations purposefully—just visible enough to be picked on for my bad skin, nonexistent fashion sense, and the biggest crime of all: I was smarter than anyone in my class and I had the nerve to be female.

That night Nick stood on his bed, stared at his poster of Dennis Rodman, and said, "Bow to those who rage on."

I went over to Nick's house after the police and all the social workers and neighbors had gone back to their lives.

At first I was going to knock on the door, but then I couldn't face Miss Gorden. Her eyes would be puffy, her face tired and sad, her body drooping. I climbed into the open hall window on the side of the house. It's the way me and Nick came in most of the time anyway.

I could hear Miss Gorden crying two rooms down. She sounded like a little kid. I almost started crying too. That would have been a good thing. That would have helped. Everybody says so. But instead I just ducked into Nick's room.

His basketball and Greenpeace posters jumped out at me and stabbed me in the heart. I used to listen to guys at school talking basketball as Nick's eyes glowed. I'd think: this time he's going to say something, talk about what happened in some game somewhere. But he never did, and none of the group ever asked.

I curled up on the bed and looked around the room. It was a friendly mess. It sat there waiting for Nick to come back to it. Maybe dream and imagine in it. I closed my eyes and in a minute was asleep.

When I woke up a few hours later, the sun was going down and Miss Gorden must have come in and taken Nick's favorite blanket off his chair and covered me in it. I pulled it over my head and inhaled

Nick, then crawled out the way I came in and walked the street-lit sidewalks.

I stood beside Miss Gorden when they put her son in the ground. I fought the urge to scream when the casket was lowered. I should have screamed.

There were eight people there: Miss Gorden, my parents and me, the school principal, and three people I'd never seen before.

Again I wanted to scream. Nobody from school came. Not one classmate. Not even to get out of those halls from hell.

Everyone cried but me.

When the service ended, Miss Gorden turned on the boom box she'd told me to bring. She sat it next to Nick's grave and smiled as "Everybody Is a Star" echoed through the cemetery. And all I could think as I got into my mom's minivan was that Nick probably wouldn't even be mad that the last time he heard his song it was on a CD.

For a week the halls and classes got quiet when I walked through them. It was like carrying a plague that would only infect others if they talked around you. They all just stayed away. I'd never gotten so much attention in my whole life by being ignored.

The second week, though, it started. The questions.

Why? And why *there*?

Did I expect it?

Did he talk about it?

I would swallow what I wanted to say and never answer.

Did they want me to put in a paragraph or less (while looking appropriately sad) how someone I loved more than anyone on the planet had lived his life, then ended it? Especially to people who couldn't give a damn whether he lived or died before he died.

Had most of the apple-smelling, Gap-wearing pack creatures ever held a single conversation with Nick?

Had any of the ones who asked me "How come?" been in a group who screamed out "Do it!" as Nick was about to let go of the rafters and swing like a rag doll in front of them?

I lasted three days in school.

> **What clues help you identify the tone and mood?**

I wrote "NICK WAS HAPPY" 3,549 times on my Grrlll Power Notebook.

Then—

Nick had been happy his whole life. He'd never had a bad day his whole life, I thought. He never seemed miserable or lonely, 'cause he had me. I thought he never minded that he was invisible. I'd always believed he never wanted to be like them, having basketball conversations and talking about what they did the night before. I guess I was wrong about it all.

Wrong that he never minded that they thought he was a sad case 'cause his best friend was a girl with bad skin who couldn't form a social sentence. Wrong that it didn't make him sad that the person he identified with most was a boy who'd died thirteen years before he was born, fighting a war that never should have been. At thirteen when Nick found out about reincarnation, he decided his uncle had come back to the world as him.

He really believed it. Believed it in his soul. Believed it more than anything he'd ever thought in his whole life, even believed it more than the thing he thought about himself being invisible.

Read-Aloud Opportunity ▶ Pass the Baton

Directions: Your teacher will select someone to read the first paragraph in "Through a Window" aloud to the class. When that person is finished, he or she names a classmate to read the next paragraph. That person reads aloud and then names the next reader, and so on, to the end of the selection.

After You Read

Converse

Directions: With your teacher's guidance, form small groups. Share opinions and ideas to complete the following activity together.

Each item that follows features a character from "Through a Window." On a scale below the name are two opposite character traits. Decide whether the character is described equally well by each trait or is more one trait than the other. Write an X on the scale to show where you place the character in relation to the traits. Then, on the lines provided, explain your choice. Use details from the story and/or personal knowledge to make the explanation clear.

1.   The speaker in "Through a Window" is . . .

angry   calm

Explanation: _____

_____

_____

_____

2.   The speaker in "Through a Window" is . . .

observant   unobservant

Explanation: _____

_____

_____

_____

3.   Nick is . . .

happy   unhappy

Explanation: _____

_____

_____

_____

4.   Nick is . . .

visible   invisible

Explanation: _____

_____

_____

_____

Connect

Directions

1. *Imagine.* Imagine that the narrator in "Kerri and Me" and the speaker in "Through a Window" board a bus and sit down next to one another. They are strangers, but they begin to talk. Based on what you know of these girls, what do you think they would talk about? What would the tone of the conversation be?

2. *Create.* With your teacher's guidance, pair up with another student. Based on your ideas in step 1, create a skit featuring the narrator from "Kerri and Me" and the speaker in "Through a Window." In your skit, show these two people getting to know each other during a bus ride. Focus on dialogue. How would they introduce themselves? What would they want to know about each other? What would they share about themselves? What tone of voice would each character use? What would be the listener's mood as the other spoke? You can make up a name for the narrator if you'd like.

3. *Perform.* Your teacher will arrange a performance schedule so that you can present your skit to the class.

Write

Directions: Write a pamphlet on grief and loss especially for young people in middle school and high school. Your pamphlet should be appropriate to give to someone like the speaker in "Through a Window" or the narrator in "Kerri and Me"—a young person who is suffering over the loss of someone dear.

1. *Set a purpose.* Decide what purpose your pamphlet will serve. For instance, do you want to educate readers, comfort readers, or offer advice? Do you want to advertise a service? Provide a Q&A or FAQs?

2. *Brainstorm.* Based on the purpose of your pamphlet, brainstorm for the main ideas you want to include.

3. *Create a mock-up.* Fold a piece of paper the way that your pamphlet will be folded. Block out sections to show how much space you'll have to address each idea. Decide on headings for the sections or other ways to set off the sections. Choose artwork, such as your own drawings or magazine cutouts, to include.

4. *Write.* Write the content of your pamphlet using your ideas from steps 1–3.

5. *Create the pamphlet.* Create the final copy of your pamphlet using your plans and writing from steps 3 and 4.

Loss

This chapter opened with an illustration of a girl looking out a window. (See page 187.) Did you notice the close-ups from this illustration scattered throughout the chapter?

What do the details of the illustration, such as the girl's expression and the flowerpot on the sill, tell you about loss? What did the stories tell you about this topic?

How does this relate to your own experience coping with the loss of someone close to you?

Chapter 10

Change

What Does This All Mean?

Being a skilled reader is like being a skilled dancer. First you learn and practice simple steps. With reading, these steps include identifying basic elements of a story, such as characters, conflict, and resolution. You learned fundamental skills like these earlier in this book. As with dancing, as you gain skill, you move from the simple to the difficult. In reading, some of the more difficult strategies include linking ideas in a passage, identifying theme, and making inferences. Finally, the skilled dancer—or reader— combines simple and difficult steps to perform challenging sequences.

This chapter shows you how to use your inference skills to **interpret figurative language**. You'll also learn to use multiple reading strategies in sequence to **ask questions to discover unstated ideas** and information. Along the way, you'll read an excerpt from a novel about a teenager who faces a major—and unwanted—change in his life.

Strategy▶
Interpret Figurative Language

Before You Read

Word Association

Directions: Use the boxes to record your reactions to the words printed in them. First, in the box for "juvenile," express ideas that the word *juvenile* brings to your mind. You may write words, phrases, or sentences. Repeat the process in the box for "delinquent." Finally, think about the two key words together—*juvenile delinquent*—and use the third box to record your ideas about that phrase.

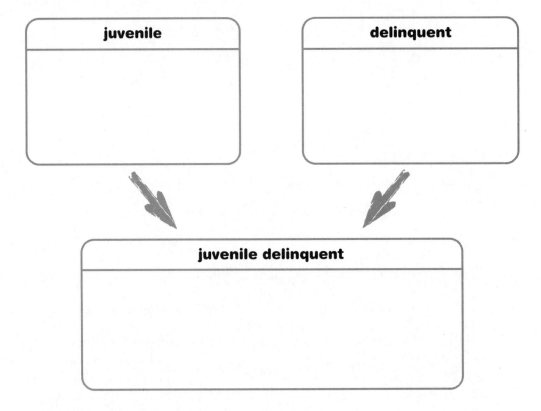

juvenile	delinquent

juvenile delinquent

Personal Opinion

Directions: An old folk saying is, "The leopard cannot change its spots." The adage (common saying) means that a person cannot change his or her basic nature. What do you think about this claim? What do you know from personal experience? On a separate sheet of paper, write two paragraphs expressing your ideas and opinions in response to the adage.

While You Read

Reading Strategy Mini-Lesson

Reading Strategy ▶ Interpret Figurative Language

The following telephone conversation uses more figurative language than you can shake a stick at. How much of it do you understand?

Zoe: Hello?

Jordon: Zoe? Your voice is music to my ears.

Zoe: Jordon? What's up?

Jordon: I am mad as a hornet.

Zoe: At me?

Jordon: Get real. I've been ripped off! My wheels are gone.

Zoe: When?

Jordon: While I was in Planet Sport. Now I'm in hot water. To get home, I'll have to hoof it. If I'm late, Mom will blow her stack. I'm dead meat! I'm roadkill!

Zoe: Don't be a drama queen. I'll be there fast as greased lightning. Just sit tight.

Jordon: You're a lifesaver. You're one in a million. You're Superman. You're . . . hello? Hello? Did you hang up?

As you can see in this conversation, **figurative language** is a way of expressing ideas creatively, not literally. Figures of speech such as "ripped off" and "hoof it" allow a speaker to communicate not just meaning but also attitude, emotion, and style. In literature, authors use figurative language to create vivid mental pictures and images of ideas. Figurative language helps set the tone of a narrative, and it makes characters unique and memorable. Figurative language helps a story come alive.

This table explains five common types of figurative language.

Figurative Language	Explanation	Examples
Simile	a comparison of unlike things that uses a word of comparison such as *like* or *as*	I could feel my heart **beating like a drum**. The old man's mind was still **sharp as a tack**.
Metaphor	a comparison in which one thing is said to be another thing; no word of comparison is used	That **car is a lemon**. Her **skin was brown leather**, her **eyes cold black pebbles**.

Figurative Language *continued*	Explanation *continued*	Example *continued*
Personification	giving human qualities to animals and nonliving things	Autumn **leaves danced** in the meadow. The **wolf said**, "I'm going to blow your house down!"
Hyperbole	exaggeration to make a point	**I could eat a horse**. I ran **halfway around the world** trying to find you.
Idiom	an expression with an understood meaning within a region or culture	The couple will **tie the knot** in a June ceremony. A good **rule of thumb** is to keep your password secret.

The key to identifying figurative language in literature is to ask, "Can these words be taken literally?" If they cannot, you are probably looking at figurative language. The key to interpreting figurative language is to use context clues. Based on context clues and personal knowledge, you can infer the most likely meaning.

The Strategy in Action

The telephone conversation between Zoe and Jordon is reprinted in the table on the next page. The version that uses figurative language is in the left column. A version that uses literal language is in the right column. Read the two versions and note the differences.

Figurative Language	Literal Language
Zoe: Hello? *Jordon: Zoe? Your **voice is music to my ears**.* *Zoe: Jordon? **What's up?*** *Jordon: I am **mad as a hornet**.* *Zoe: At me?* *Jordon: **Get real**. I've been **ripped off**! My **wheels** are gone.* *Zoe: When?* *Jordon: While I was in Planet Sport. Now I'm **in hot water**. To get home, I'll have to **hoof it**. If I'm late, Mom will **blow her stack**. I'm **dead meat**! I'm **roadkill**!* *Zoe: Don't **be a drama queen**. I'll be there **fast as greased lightning**. Just **sit tight**.* *Jordon: **You're a lifesaver. You're one in a million. You're Superman**. You're . . . hello? Hello? Did you hang up?*	*Zoe: Hello?* *Jordon: Zoe? **I am happy to hear your voice**. Zoe: Jordon? **What is happening?*** *Jordon: I am **very angry**.* *Zoe: At me?* *Jordon: **Don't suggest things that aren't believable**. I've been **robbed**! My **bicycle** is gone.* *Zoe: When?* *Jordon: While I was in Planet Sport. Now I'm in **trouble**. To get home, I'll have to **walk**. If I'm late, Mom will **become very angry. My situation is hopeless! I have been defeated by this situation!*** *Zoe: Don't **be overly dramatic**. I'll be there **quickly**. Just **wait**.* *Jordon: You're **someone who solved a difficult problem for me**. You're **very special**. You're **a person with extraordinary powers**. You're . . . hello? Hello? Did you hang up?*

Give It a Try

Interpret Figurative Language

Directions: Read the excerpt from *Touching Spirit Bear* on pages 217–219. Use the following table to interpret figurative language as you read. The first four items contain examples of figurative language from the selection for you to interpret. For items 5 and 6, list and interpret your *own* examples of figurative language that you find in the passage.

Hint: The passage contains one example of personification and one example of hyperbole. It contains many idioms, similes, and metaphors.

Interpreting Figurative Language
in *Touching Spirit Bear*

Figurative Language	Interpretation
Example: Overhead, a gray-matted <u>sky hung like a bad omen</u>. (paragraph 1)	*Example:* The sky made it look like something bad would happen.
1. Two men accompanied Cole on this final <u>leg of his journey</u>. (paragraph 2)	
2. He was <u>built like a bulldog with lazy eyes</u>. (paragraph 2)	
3. Garvey pretended to be a friend, but Cole knew <u>he was nothing more than a paid baby-sitter</u>. (paragraph 2)	
4. "<u>Get real</u>, old man," Cole answered. (paragraph 5)	
5. *Your example:*	
6. *Your example:*	

Reading Selection

from Touching Spirit Bear

by Ben Mikaelsen

Cole Matthews knelt defiantly in the bow of the aluminum skiff as he faced forward into a cold September wind. Worn steel handcuffs bit at his wrists each time the small craft slapped into another wave. Overhead, a gray-matted sky hung like a bad omen. Cole strained at the cuffs even though he had agreed to wear them until he was freed on the island to begin his banishment. Agreeing to spend a whole year alone in Southeast Alaska had been his only way of avoiding a jail cell in Minneapolis.

Two men accompanied Cole on this final leg of the journey. In the middle sat Garvey, the gravelly-voiced, wisecracking Indian parole officer from Minneapolis. Garvey said he was a Tlingit Indian, pronouncing *Tlingit* proudly with a clicking of his tongue as if saying "Klingkit." He was built like a bulldog with lazy eyes. Cole didn't trust Garvey. He didn't trust anyone who wasn't afraid of him. Garvey pretended to be a friend, but Cole knew he was nothing more than a paid baby-sitter. This week his job was escorting a violent juvenile offender from Minneapolis to Seattle, then to Ketchikan, Alaska, where they boarded a big silver floatplane to the Tlingit village of Drake. Now they were headed for some island in the middle of nowhere.

In the rear of the skiff sat Edwin, a quiet, potbellied Tlingit elder who had helped arrange Cole's banishment. He steered the boat casually, a faded blue T-shirt and baggy jeans his only protection against the wind. Deep-set eyes made it hard to tell what Edwin was thinking. He stared forward with a steely patience, like a wolf waiting. Cole didn't trust him either.

It was Edwin who had built the shelter and made all the preparations on the island where Cole was to stay. When he first met Edwin in Drake, the gruff elder took one look and pointed a finger at him. "Go put your clothes on inside out," he ordered.

"Get real, old man," Cole answered.

"You'll wear them reversed for the first two weeks of your banishment to show humility and shame," Edwin said, his voice hard as stone. Then he turned and shuffled up the dock toward his old rusty pickup.

Cole hesitated, eyeing the departing elder.

"Just do it," Garvey warned.

Still standing on the dock in front of everyone, Cole smirked as he undressed. He refused to turn his back as he slowly pulled each piece inside out—even his underwear. Villagers watched from the shore until he finished changing.

Bracing himself now against the heavy seas, Cole held that same smirk. His blue jeans, heavy wool shirt, and rain jacket chafed his skin, but it didn't matter. He would have worn a cowbell around his neck if it had meant avoiding jail. He wasn't a Tlingit Indian. He was an innocent-looking, baby-faced fifteen-year-old from Minneapolis who had been in trouble with the law half his life. Everyone thought he felt sorry for what he had done, and going to this island was his way of making things right.

Nothing could be further from the truth. To Cole, this was just another big game. With salt air biting at his face, he turned and glanced at Edwin. The elder eyed him back with a dull stare. Anger welled up inside Cole. He hated that stupid stare. Pretending to aim toward the waves, he spit so the wind would catch the thick saliva and carry it back.

The spit caught Edwin squarely and dragged across his faded shirt. Edwin casually lifted an oil rag from the bottom of the skiff and wiped away the slime, then tossed the rag back under his seat and again fixed his eyes on Cole.

Cole feigned surprise as he if had made a horrible mistake, then twisted at the handcuffs again. What was this old guy's problem anyway? The elder acted fearless, but he had to be afraid of something. Everyone in the world was afraid of something.

Cole thought back to all the people at home who had tried to help him over the years. He hated their fake concern. They didn't really care what happened to him. They were gutless—he could see it in

> Look for examples of figurative language.

their eyes. They were afraid, glad to be rid of him. They pretended to help only because they didn't know what else to do.

For years, "help" had meant sending him to drug counseling and anger therapy sessions. Every few months, Cole found himself being referred to someone else. He discovered early on that "being referred" was the adult term for passing the buck. Already he had seen the inside of a dozen police stations, been through as many counselors, a psychologist, several detention centers, and two residential treatment centers.

Each time he got into trouble, he was warned to shape up because this was his last chance. Even the day he left for the island, several of those who gathered to see him off, including his parents, had warned him, "Don't screw up. This is your last chance." Cole braced himself for the next big wave. Whatever happened, he would always count on having one more *last* chance.

Not that it really mattered. He had no intention of ever honoring the contract he agreed to during the Circle Justice meetings. As soon as they left him alone, this silly game would end. Circle Justice was a bunch of bull. They were crazy if they thought he was going to spend a whole year of his life like some animal, trapped on a remote Alaskan island.

to be continued

Read-Aloud Opportunity ▶ Key Paragraphs

Directions

1. *Read silently.* On your own, go back over the excerpt from *Touching Spirit Bear* on pages 217–219. As you read, pay attention to details that bring Cole Matthews alive on the page.

2. *Choose a paragraph.* Choose one paragraph that was especially helpful in making Cole Matthews seem like a real person to you. Underline the details (or jot details on sticky notes) that describe or reveal the character. Practice reading this paragraph aloud.

3. *Read aloud.* With your teacher's guidance, form small groups. Read the paragraph you chose in step 2 aloud to the group. Point out the details in the paragraph that make Cole Matthews come alive. In response, group members may ask you questions or make comments.

After You Read

Converse

Directions

1. *Discuss.* With your teacher's guidance, form small groups. Together, find details in the story to answer the question *What is happening to whom, and why is it happening?* On the lines below, write one to three sentences that answer this question.

_____

_____

_____

_____

_____

_____

2. *Regroup and share.* Regroup with the entire class. Share your answer from step 1 and answer questions and respond to comments from classmates. Listen as other groups share their answers from step 1 and notice how each answer is similar to and/or different from yours. Why do you think differences among answers occurred?

Connect

Directions: On a sheet of paper, draw a stick figure to represent Cole Matthews. Think about what the story has revealed so far about this character. Around the sides of the stick figure, write at least *five* statements using **figurative language** that describe Cole. For example, how would you describe his heart? His mind? His hands? His feet? His eyes? You'll have to get creative—for example, you could say he has feet of clay, which means he is imperfect.

Directions: Choose option A or B. Challenge: Try to use figurative language in your response.

A. Based on what you've read about Cole Matthews so far, what do you think he needs to change about himself? Scan the excerpt on pages 217–219, looking for clues to Cole's ideas, attitudes, habits, actions, and plans. On a separate sheet of paper, write two or three paragraphs in which you

- use details from the story to explain two things that Cole should change about himself
- explain why you think he should change these aspects of himself

   OR

B. Based on what you've read about Cole Matthews so far, do you think he *will* change? Scan the excerpt on pages 217–219, looking for clues to Cole's ideas, attitudes, habits, actions, and plans. On a separate sheet of paper, write two or three paragraphs in which you

- use details from the story to explain what and why you think Cole *will* change
- explain how you think he will change

Strategy ▶
Ask Questions to Discover Unstated Ideas

In Chapter 1, you learned to ask yourself questions as you read a passage to monitor your comprehension. In Chapter 2, you learned to ask questions to make sure you notice meaningful details in the passage. A third reason to **ask questions** is to help yourself infer ideas that are not stated directly. For instance, you might ask why a character is angry all the time. You might ask why the story events happen in the time and place that they do. You might ask why the author uses a certain key word so frequently. In questioning the text in this way, you are not just an active reader. You are a curious reader.

Before You Read

Thought Grid

Directions: Complete the following thought grid about justice.

What is justice?	What is the purpose of justice?	Do we live in a just world?
_____ _____	_____ _____ _____	_____ _____ _____
What is at least one antonym of *justice*? _____ _____ _____	**justice**	**What are synonyms of *justice*?** _____ _____ _____
Does everyone deserve justice, no matter what? _____ _____ _____	**Draw a sketch to represent *justice* in picture form.**	**What is the criminal justice system?** _____ _____ _____

Set a Purpose for Reading

Directions: Think about the first excerpt you read from *Touching Spirit Bear*. What is one thing you hope to find out when you continue reading the story? Write your answer below.

In the next part of *Touching Spirit Bear*, I hope to find out _____

_____

While You Read

Reading Strategy ▶ Ask Questions to Discover Unstated ideas

At the heart of every question asked is an attitude of curiosity. "Why?" you wonder. "When?" or "Where?" or "How?" By **asking questions** as you read, you allow your curiosity to lead you to insights you would not have noticed without asking—and answering—questions.

To infer unstated ideas from a passage, you must not only ask questions about the passage; you must answer your own questions too. To do so, you make lots of connections—between details in the passage, between the passage and your personal knowledge, between the passage and other things you've read, and between the passage and the world around you. (You may recall the reading strategy of making connections, discussed in Chapter 5.)

Asking questions, making connections, and inferring ideas may sound challenging. But you have already practiced these reading strategies separately in other parts of this book. The box shows how you can use the strategies together.

> ### Ask Questions to Discover Unstated Ideas
>
> 1. Ask a question.
> 2. Find relevant details in the passage.
> 3. Make a connection to other stated details, personal knowledge, other passages, or the world.
> 4. Use the information from steps 2 and 3 to infer an idea or conclusion.

Watch This!

The Strategy in Action

Think again of the movie "Spider-Man." In it, Spider-Man is bitten by a spider and gains special powers. At first, he wants to use his powers to make money so that he can win the affection of the girl he likes. Later, however, when his uncle is killed, he decides to use his power to fight evil.

As you watch this part of the movie, many questions may occur to you. You may wonder, "Why does Peter initially want to use his powers to make money? Why does Peter decide to fight evil?" The following table shows how you can question the story to discover the unstated reasons why.

Question	Story Details	My Connection	Answer
Why does Peter initially want to use his powers to make money?	The movie shows that he has a big crush on a girl, Mary Jane.	A lot of people I know do things to try to impress people they like.	Maybe Peter thinks that if he has a lot of money, Mary Jane will like him.
Why does Peter decide to fight evil?	The movie shows how bad Peter feels when his uncle is murdered. The movie also shows the uncle's warning that with "great power comes great responsibility."	A lot of people learn lessons the hard way. They miss an opportunity to do something, and then they vow to change after that.	Peter must feel guilty for not saving his uncle, and he realizes that he should be doing more with his powers than just trying to make money.

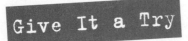

Ask Questions to Discover Unstated Ideas

Directions: Read the second excerpt from *Touching Spirit Bear* on pages 226–230. Use the table on the next page to infer unstated ideas or conclusions about this selection. Use words, phrases, and/or complete sentences to fill in the table.

**Asking Questions
About *Touching Spirit Bear***

Question	Story Details	My Connection	Answer
Question 1			
Question 2			
Question 3			
Question 4			

Reading Selection

from Touching Spirit Bear

by Ben Mikaelsen

continued from page 219

Cole twisted at the handcuffs again. Last year at this time, he had never even heard of Circle Justice—he hadn't heard of it until his latest arrest for breaking into a hardware store. After robbing the place, he had totally trashed it.

The police might not have caught him, but after a week passed, he bragged about the break-in at school. When someone ratted on him, the police questioned Cole. He denied the break-in, of course, and then he beat up the boy who had turned him in.

The kid, Peter Driscal, was a ninth grader Cole had picked on many times before just for the fun of it. Still, no one ratted on Cole Matthews without paying the price. That day, he caught up to Peter in the hallway at school. "You're a dead man," he warned the skinny red-haired boy, giving him a hard shove. He laughed when he saw fear in Peter's eyes.

Later, after school, Cole cornered Peter outside in the parking lot. With anger that had been brewing all day, he attacked him and started hitting him hard in the face with his bare fists. Peter was no match, and soon Cole had pounded him bloody. A dozen students stood watching. When Peter tried to escape, he tripped and fell to the ground. Cole jumped on him again and started smashing his head against the sidewalk. It took six other students to finally pull him away. By then Peter was cowering on the blood-smeared sidewalk, sobbing. Cole laughed and spit at him even as he was held back. Nobody crossed Cole Matthews and got away with it.

Because of his vicious attack on Peter Driscal, Cole had been kept at a detention center while the courts decided what to do with him. His white-walled room was bare except for a bed with a gray blanket, a toilet without a cover, a shelf for clothes, a cement table, and a barred window facing onto the center group area. The place smelled like cleaning disinfectant.

Each night guards locked the room's thick steel door. They called this detention space a room, but Cole knew it was really a jail cell. A room didn't need a locked steel door. During the day, guards allowed Cole to go into the central group area with other juveniles if he wanted to. He could read, watch TV, or talk. They expected him to do schoolwork with a tutor that came each day. What a joke. This was no school, and he was no student. Cole did as little as absolutely possible, keeping to himself. The other detainees were a bunch of losers.

Cole figured he wouldn't even be here if Peter Driscal had known how to fight back. Instead, Peter was hospitalized. Doctors' reports warned he might suffer permanent damage. "Serves him right," Cole mumbled when he was first told of Peter's condition.

What angered Cole the most after this latest arrest were his parents. In the past they had always come running with a lawyer, offering to pay damages and demanding his release. They had enough money and connections to move mountains. Besides, they had a reputation to protect. What parent wanted the world to know their son was a juvenile delinquent? All Cole did was pretend he was sorry for a few days till things blew over. But that was how it had been in the past, before his parents got divorced.

This time he hadn't been freed. He was told that because of his past record and the violence of this attack, he would be kept locked up while prosecutors filed a motion to transfer him to adult court. Even Nathaniel Blackwood, the high-priced criminal defense lawyer hired by his dad, told Cole he might be tried as an adult. If convicted, he'd be sent to prison.

Ask questions as you read. What are you curious about in this section?

Cole couldn't believe his parents were letting this happen to him. What jerks! He hated his parents. His mom acted like a scared Barbie doll, always looking good but never fighting back or standing up to anyone. His dad was a bullheaded drinker with a temper. He figured everything was Cole's fault. Why wasn't his room clean? Why hadn't he emptied the garbage? Why hadn't he mowed the lawn? Why was he even alive?

"I never want to see your ugly faces again," Cole shouted at the lawyer and his parents after finding out he wouldn't be released. But still his parents tried to see him. Because of their divorce, they visited separately. That's how much they thought about themselves and about him, Cole thought. They couldn't even swallow their dumb pride and visit together.

During each visit, Cole relaxed on his bed and pretended to read a newspaper, completely ignoring them. He liked watching his parents, especially his dad, squirm and get frustrated. Some days his dad got so mad, he turned beet red and twitched because he couldn't lay a finger on Cole with the guards watching.

Finally his parents quit trying to visit. Even Nathaniel Blackwood quit stopping by except when hearings and depositions required his presence. Cole didn't like the lawyer. Blackwood was a stiff man and spoke artificially, as if he were addressing an audience through a microphone. Cole swore he wore starch on everything. Judging by how he walked, that included his underwear.

The only person who insisted on visiting regularly was Garvey, the stocky youth probation officer, who stopped by the detention center almost daily.

Cole couldn't figure Garvey out. He knew the probation officer was super busy, so why did he visit so often? What was his angle? Everybody had an angle—something they wanted. Until Cole could figure out what Garvey wanted, he resented the visits—he didn't need a friend or a baby-sitter.

During one visit, Garvey asked casually, "I know you're in control, Champ, but would you ever consider applying for Circle Justice?"

"What's Circle Justice?"

"It's a healing form of justice practiced by native cultures for thousands of years."

"I'm no Indian," Cole said.

Garvey spoke patiently. "You don't have to be Native American or First Nation. Anybody can love, forgive, and heal. Nobody has a corner on that market."

"What's in it for me?"

Garvey shook his head. "If you kill my cat, normally the police fine you and that's it. We still hate each other, I still feel bad about my cat, and you're angry because you have to pay a fine. In Circle Justice, you sign a healing contract. You might agree to help me pick out a new kitten and care for it as part of the sentencing."

"Why would I want to take care of a dumb cat?"

"Because you've caused my cat and me harm. By doing something for me and another cat, you help make things right again."

"What if I don't care about you and your dumb cat?"

"Then do it for yourself. You're also a victim. Something terrible has happened to you to make you want to kill a poor small animal."

Cole shrugged. "Feeding a dumb cat beats paying a fine."

Garvey smiled and clapped Cole on the back. "You just don't get it, do you, Champ?"

Cole ducked away from Garvey. He hated being called Champ. And he hated being touched. Nobody ever touched him except to hit him. That's how it had been as long as he could remember.

"Circle Justice tries to heal, not punish," Garvey explained. "Your lawyer might take you to a zoo to help you appreciate animals more. The prosecutor might have you watch a veterinarian operate for a day to realize the value of life. The judge might help you on the weekend to make birdhouses as a repayment to the animal kingdom for something you destroyed. Even neighbors might help in some way."

"They actually do this stuff here in Minneapolis?"

Garvey nodded. "It's a new trial program. Other towns and cities are trying it, too."

"Why go to so much trouble?"

"To heal. Justice should heal, not punish. If you kill my cat, you need to become more sensitive to animals. You and I need to be friends, and I need to forgive you to get over my anger. That's Circle Justice. Everybody is part of the healing, including people from the community—anybody who cares. But healing is much harder than standard punishment. Healing requires taking responsibility for your actions."

Cole bit at his lip. "So would this get me out of going to jail?"

"It isn't about avoiding jail," Garvey said. "You go to jail angry, you stay angry. Go with love, that's how you come back. This is all about *how* you do something, not *what* you do. Even jail can be positive if you go in with a good heart. I will say this, however. Usually the jail sentence, if there is one, is reduced under Circle Justice."

That's all Cole needed to hear. He knew what game to play. "How do I get into this Circle Justice stuff?" he asked innocently.

Garvey placed a hand on Cole's shoulder. "I'll get you an application," he said, "but you're the one who starts the process in your heart." He tapped Cole's chest. "If you don't want change, this will never work."

Cole forced himself not to pull away from Garvey's hand. "I really do want change," he said, using the innocent childish voice that had served him well countless times before.

Garvey nodded. "Okay, let's see if you're serious. I'll help you out with the application."

After Garvey left the detention center that day, Cole jabbed his fist into the air. "Yes!" he exclaimed. The world was made up of suckers and fools, and today Garvey was at the top of the heap.

Read-Aloud Opportunity ▶ Attention-Grabbing Paragraphs

Directions

1. *Read silently.* On your own, go back over the excerpt from *Touching Spirit Bear* on pages 226–230. Place a check mark (or sticky note) next to paragraphs that grabbed your attention and piqued your curiosity about Cole, an event, Circle Justice, or something else.

2. *Choose a paragraph.* Choose one paragraph that made you especially curious to know more. Practice reading this paragraph aloud.

3. *Read aloud.* With your teacher's guidance, form small groups. Read the paragraph you chose in step 2 aloud to the group. Tell the group what the paragraph made you curious about—what it made you want to know. In response, group members may ask you questions or make comments.

After You Read

 **Converse**

Directions: The following statements express ideas about characters in *Touching Spirit Bear.* You may or may not agree with each statement. Your teacher will read each statement aloud and ask for a show of hands. Raise your hand at the appropriate time to show that you agree or disagree with the statement. Then share your reasons for your point of view and listen to the reasons other people give for their responses.

1. Cole is just a misunderstood kid.
2. Cole's dad caused Cole to become a delinquent.
3. Cole deserved prison, not Circle Justice.
4. Cole's parents do not care about him anymore.
5. Circle Justice will heal Cole.

 **Connect**

Directions: Asking Cole Matthews to reform is like asking a leopard to change its spots—in other words, for Cole to do so would go against impulses that seem to come naturally to him. Think of a change that you want to make in yourself that seems equally difficult. Perhaps it is trying to change your study habits, lose weight, stop lying, accept your new stepbrother or stepsister, or something else equally challenging. Then write responses to the following prompts:

1. The change I want to make is _____

2. This change seems hard to make because _____

_____

3. When other people suggest that I make this change, I feel _____

_____

4. It would be easier to make this change if _____

_____

5. Ultimately, I think that I will/will not (circle one) make this change because

_____

_____

 **Write**

Directions: Imagine that you are Garvey, the probation officer assigned to Cole Matthews. Prepare a case file using the form on the next page. Under Comments, write ideas, information, and conclusions that you have inferred about Cole.

CONFIDENTIAL

Case File

State of Minnesota

Juvenile Justice System

Date: _____

Probation officer: _____

Subject's name: _____

Charge of delinquency (the offense): _____

_____

_____

Subject's response to the charge: _____

_____

_____

Comments: _____

_____

_____

_____

_____

_____

_____

_____

_____

_____

Reflections

Change

This chapter opened with an illustration showing a teenage boy sitting on a chair in a hallway. (See page 211.) Did you notice the close-ups from this illustration scattered throughout the chapter?

What do you think the teen in the illustration is thinking about, and where do you think he is? Do you think he is similar to or different from Cole?

What connections can you make to the teen in the picture or to Cole?

Chapter 11

Parent-Child Relationships

Critical Comparisons and Analyses

Critical is one of those words that have many variations in meaning, depending on context. Most often, perhaps, we think of *critical* as meaning "faultfinding." In that case, to think critically is to search out flaws. But this is just one meaning of the word. In the study of literature, to think critically means to make informed, skilled judgments about aspects of a passage.

This chapter shows you how to use critical-thinking skills to **make comparisons and contrasts about unstated ideas** in a passage. It also teaches you how to **analyze conflict and resolution** in a narrative. You'll work with a story about a difficult parent-child relationship.

Strategy▶
Compare and Contrast Unstated Ideas

Before You Read

(**IMO Table**)

Directions: With your teacher's guidance, form groups of two or three people. Together, complete the following steps.

1. *Sort out the clue words.* The clue words in the table below are taken from the passage you are going to read. Each word or phrase is part of the Characters, Setting, Problem, or Outcome in the story. Using each word or phrase only once, write the words in the box where you think they best fit. The Unknown Words box is for words whose meaning you do not know.

2. *Form an opinion.* Based on how you sorted the clue words, decide what will likely happen in the story. Using as many of the words as possible, write your opinion on the lines provided.

3. *Ask questions.* The clue words and your prediction may have left you wondering about certain words or details. In the To find out box, jot down what you want to find out when you read the selection.

IMO Table
To predict what will happen, in my opinion, in "Visit" by Walter Dean Myers

Clue Words		
round prison clock	mortally wounded	going down wrong
flaky dudes	brutal	still-unlined forehead
blood	good-bye	grim theater of our fears
hulking silence	father	
guard	visitors	

IMO Table *(continued)*		
Characters	**Setting**	**Problem**
Outcome	**Unknown Words**	**To find out . . .**

In my opinion, what will happen is . . . _____

_____

_____

_____

_____

_____

Idea Map

Directions: What are some of the things that you think are most important to a parent-child relationship? Perhaps attitudes such as respect or tolerance are important, or actions such as hugs or help doing something. Use the main idea bubble on the next page to create an idea map about parent-child relationships. One idea has been added to get you started.

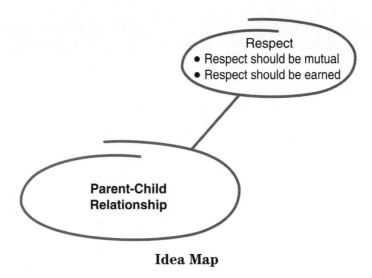

Respect
- Respect should be mutual
- Respect should be earned

Parent-Child
Relationship

Idea Map

While You Read

Reading Strategy Mini-Lesson

Reading Strategy ▶ Compare and Contrast Unstated Ideas

In Chapter 7, you learned to compare and contrast story characters using a Venn diagram. In the diagram, you listed ways that two characters were alike and ways that they were different. When making these comparisons and contrasts, you relied heavily on details that were stated in the story. In Chapters 8 through 10, you learned to look past the stated details in a story to infer ideas and draw conclusions.

Now you can draw upon all of those skills to **compare and contrast** ideas that you infer from a story. For example, you could compare and contrast

- the moods or attitudes of two characters
- the mood of the story at the beginning and the mood at the end
- two characters' relationship long ago and their relationship now
- a character's view of himself or herself and the world's (or another character's) view of that character
- the tone and the mood of the story

Let's say, for example, that you want to compare and contrast the moods of the father and the son in "Visit" by Walter Dean Myers, the story you will read in this chapter. You would complete the following steps.

Compare and Contrast Unstated Ideas	Example Using "Visit"
1. Study the story to find stated details.	Find details and information in the story about the father's mood and the son's mood.
2. Consider personal knowledge.	Think about what you know of moods, how people express the mood they're in, and how sometimes people try to disguise their mood.
3. Make inferences and draw conclusions.	Infer what kind of mood each character is in. Draw conclusions about the moods.
4. Make comparisons and contrasts.	Describe how the two characters' moods are alike and how they are different. Use examples from the story and your own reasons to support and clarify the points you make about the characters' moods.

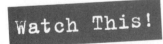

The Strategy in Action

The table on the next page shows an example of how a reader might use the four steps above to compare and contrast the father's mood and the son's mood in the first half of "Visit."

As you read the table, you'll get a sneak review of what "Visit" is about.

Comparing and Contrasting
Characters' Moods in "Visit"

Sample Thought Process

1. Study the story to find stated details.

father:

"I try to smile"

"I lie." (repeated in story)

"We watch the clock"

"My stomach turns."

"Bless me, father, for I have sinned"

son:

"eyes are downcast"

"voice trails off"

"looks away, toward nothing"

"shifts his body"

"glances up at the clock"

"tears streaming down his face"

"voice is so quiet, so childlike"

2. Consider personal knowledge.

about the father's details:

When someone forces a smile and lies, he is putting up a front for some reason. He is covering up how he really feels.

When I don't want to be somewhere, like in class, I watch the clock. This also relates to struggling to get through the minutes and wanting the time to be over. I just want out of there!

People who are religious ask for God's blessing when they know they have done something wrong.

about the son's details:

Crying, in my experience, is due to an overflow of emotion, when words aren't enough. Also, in my experience, crying usually makes you feel better because you let all the emotion out.

From what I know of body language, a person feels uncertain and insecure when he doesn't meet your eyes, shifts around, and lets his sentences trail off.

3. Make inferences and draw conclusions.

Overall, the father's mood is <u>regret</u>. He regrets not being a good father to his son. The son's mood is mostly <u>dejection</u>. He feels dejected about what is happening to him.

4. Make comparisons and contrasts.

Ways their moods are alike:

The moods are alike because they both contain sorrow. The father is sad because he wasn't a good father. The son is sad because he never got to know his

Ways their moods are different:

The father's mood of regret shows that he wishes he could change things in the past. He understands that he was not a good father. In contrast, the son

Sample Thought Process
continued

Ways their moods are alike
continued:

father. They are both sad because the son is about to die.

In their own ways, they both have sorrow in their overall mood. The father feels sorrowful regret, and the son feels sorrowful dejection.

Ways their moods are different,
continued:

says that he himself is not a bad person. He is dejected about his fate, but he isn't regretful about the kind of person he is.

The son's dejection shows that he is in a powerless position. He can no longer make his own choices. He is unsure of his relationship with his father. In contrast, instead of feeling dejected about things, the father wants forgiveness for what he did wrong.

Give It a Try

Compare and Contrast Unstated Ideas

Directions: Now read the first half of "Visit" on pages 240–243, and make your own comparisons and contrasts about unstated ideas. Choose one of the following to compare and contrast:

- the father and son's relationship long ago and their relationship now
- the son's view of himself and the world's (or his father's) view of him
- the tone and the mood of the story

On your own paper, follow the steps you learned and compare and contrast the ideas you chose from the bulleted list above.

Reading Selection

Visit

by Walter Dean Myers

"You have thirty minutes," the guard says. He nods toward a gray table with straight-backed chairs on either side.

I start to sit as the other door, the one not for visitors, opens. I try to smile as he walks toward me. *Oh, God, he is so young.*

"Hey, what's happening?" A smile flickers across the broad, brown face. There are pimples on his forehead.

We shake hands. It is the first time we have touched for twenty years. He sits. I sit.

"Have you heard anything?" I ask.

"Nah. How you doing?" His eyes dart away.

"I'm okay."

"I guess you're surprised to hear from me?"

The smile again flickers across his face. His eyes are downcast.

"A little," I say.

"I didn't have nobody else to put on the list."

"Hey, it's all good," I hear myself saying. "So, how are you doing?"

"I'm watching the clock, and the clock is watching me," he says.

"I know what you mean," I lie. I don't know what he means, not inside, not the way he feels.

"They wouldn't let me bring anything."

"I don't need anything," he says. "I was thinking . . ." His voice trails off, he looks away, toward nothing, toward the gray cinder-block wall. There are heavy seconds of silence.

"It's been a long time," I say.

"I didn't remember how you looked," he says.

His eyes search my face. He is searching for recognition.

"It was at Johnnie Mae's house," I say. "She had a cold and you had a cold. I went down to the drugstore for some cold medicine."

"How old was I?" he asks.

"Three? Maybe three, or two," I answer.

"More than twenty years ago."

"A long time."

"Well, what happened was that things went all right for a while," he says. He shifts his body. "Then they got confused."

I nod. He has a story to tell. I'll listen.

Another moment of silence. On the wall, the round prison clock looks down like the true face of God.

"Where were you living?" I ask.

"On 141st Street," he says. "You know where the building fell down?"

"Yes," I lie.

"We were living down the street from there," he said. "Near the playground. And she was on the pipe."

Johnnie Mae. I hadn't seen her in years. Dark. Wide-eyed. Wide-hipped . . .

"What did you do?"

"Hung out mostly," he says. "I wasn't doing right, you know." *Confession.*

"Sometimes it's hard to do the right thing," I say.

"No, man, you can do the right thing if you want to."

He glances up at the clock. It's four o'clock.

"So . . ." he continues. "I got in with this bunch of dudes. Flaky dudes, really. We did a little of this and a little of that. Sold some weed, did some jacking. Some jive get-overs. Nothing real—you know what I mean?"

"Yeah."

> **Remember to compare and also contrast as you read.**

"Then one day this dude calls me up and wants to know if I wanted to get paid for nothing." He is talking faster. "I asked him what he meant and he said he had a walk through and all he needed was a lookout. I knew you didn't get paid for nothing, but I went along with the program. I was wrong right there."
Bless me, father, for I have sinned.

"Sometimes," I say, "you can't tell . . .."

"So, what did you think when you heard about it?"

"I was disappointed," I lie. I didn't hear about it. I read about the appeal that was turned down in the newspaper on the A train going up to Harlem. There was no connection between us, no father-and-son thing that would have sent the calls from mothers, grandmothers, brothers buzzing through the city streets. "I was hoping it wasn't true."

We watch the clock, the clock watches us.

"It was supposed to be a push in," he continues. "He said this old woman had a heavy stash up in her mattress. He was going to push in and take the money, and we were going just to hang out like nothing happened because she never came out of the house and wouldn't know who we were if she saw us."

"Just the two of you?"

"Yeah. He was going to do the thing and I was just supposed to sit out on the steps and keep an eye out for people coming off the elevator. But he took a few hits—I think he was using crack or something—to get his thing together before he went in. Then he went in while I was out sitting on the stairs. Then he come out and said that the thing was going down wrong. He needed me in there."

"You went in?"

"Yeah. I should have split right then and there, but I went in," he says. "The old woman was laying on the floor, all angled up and moaning. And there was her husband, he's sitting in a wheelchair, shaking and carrying on and crying about his wife."

"Oh, God."

"I know you hate to hear that," he says. "You didn't think I was going to ever get into nothing like that, right?"

"I was hoping . . ."

"Randy—that's the guy I'm backing up—he didn't know anything about her husband even being there. And we're sitting there wondering what to do."

"Why didn't you just walk away?"

"Because the woman looks like she's dead," he says. "According to the medical examiner, she was, like, mortally wounded."

The missing years take invisible shape and sit between us. I keep my eyes away from the clock.

"And?" I ask.

"Then Randy says we got to off the old man. There's a hammer in the kitchen. You know, if he had shot him and there wasn't so much . . ."

Pause. My stomach turns. *Flesh of my flesh. Blood of my blood.*

"So much blood?" I had read the newspaper accounts.

"Yeah. Maybe it would have been different," he says. "It would have been the same, but not so, like, brutal."

"Yeah."

"You know, I'm sorry about this whole thing," he says. "They said I didn't have no remorse but, really, I was in such a deep shock kind of thing, I didn't even know what I was saying or doing."

"It was seven years ago," I said. "You were only seventeen."

"Eighteen," he corrects me.

"Eighteen."

"I'm sorry, too," I say. The hulking silence leans forward, peering into our faces . . .

"Anyway, Randy was tripping . . ." he continues, needing to go on with his story.

"You were in the apartment . . ."

"And I'm like shocked because I never saw so much blood—no, it's like I've never seen people hurt like that. One minute they're like people and then they're like whimpering and crying and they're something else."

"That had to be hard."

"That's not me, man," he says. "Hurting people like that. That's not me."

He looks away. There are tears streaming down his face, down the cheekbones that mimic mine, diagonally down along the light brown jawline that is mine, that is the jawline of the grandfather he has never seen.

"I know it's not you," I say.

"So Randy and I split and I don't want anything to do with him because the whole thing is foul and I know we've blown the set big time," he says. "You know what I mean?"

"Yeah."

"But it's done, man," he says. "Ain't no rerun, ain't no thinking about how it should have ended."

"It's done," I echo.

"And it's me."

The voice is so quiet, so childlike. We are in the giddy vortex of what might have been, trying to catch the long-past moment.

"And it's you, son."

to be continued

Read-Aloud Opportunity ▶ Dramatic Reading

Directions

1. *Pair.* With your teacher's guidance, pair up with another student. Together, choose a section of the story that reveals something important about the father and son's relationship. Quietly, practice reading aloud just the dialogue in this section, with each of you taking a different part (the father or the son).

2. *Perform.* Your teacher will give you an opportunity to perform your dramatic reading for the class. After you and your partner read your chosen section aloud, explain what you think the section reveals about the father and son's relationship.

After You Read

 **Converse**

Directions

1. *Write.* At the top of a sheet of paper, write one discussion prompt or question about "Visit" that you think would trigger an interesting exchange of ideas.

2. *Lead.* With your teacher's guidance, form small groups. Read your discussion prompt to your group and lead a five-minute discussion about it. As discussion leader, you may need to explain your prompt further, answer questions about your point of view, encourage others to share their ideas, and keep the discussion on track. On your paper, jot down notes about the ideas exchanged.

3. *Discuss.* Listen as others in your group read their discussion prompts, and respond by sharing your ideas and opinions.

 **Connect**

Directions: With your teacher's guidance, form small groups. Connect to "Visit" by comparing and contrasting details in the story to your experiences in real life. Use one of the connection prompts on the next page to get your ideas flowing, and share your ideas with the group. In response, group members may ask you questions and offer their opinions.

Connection Prompts

The son reminds me of . . .

The father reminds me of . . .

The son's situation is similar to . . .

I also . . .

I never . . .

This story makes me feel . . .

This reminds me of . . .

Directions

1. *Review.* Review the idea map you created about parent-child relationships on page 236.

2. *Create.* Create another idea map, this time focusing on the parent-child relationship in the first half of "Visit." Use the map to show the nature of the relationship these two characters have.

3. *Write.* Write three to five paragraphs in which you compare and contrast the ideas in the two idea maps. Offer your opinion or judgment about the parent-child relationship in the story, using the ideas in your own idea map as the measuring stick.

Strategy▶

Analyze Conflict and Resolution

In Chapter 3, you learned to *identify* the conflict and the resolution in a narrative. Doing so helped you answer such questions as "What happened?" and "Why?" and "How did it all turn out?" Once you've asked and answered these questions, you are ready to think more critically about the plot of the story. This section of the chapter shows you how to ***analyze* conflict and resolution** in a narrative.

Before You Read

Making Predictions

Directions: What do you think will happen in the second half of "Visit"? Write your predictions below.

_____

_____

_____

Freewrite

Directions: Think about a time you wished you could say something to someone, but you had trouble expressing it. In a journal or on a sheet of paper, reflect on the situation. What were you holding in, and why? Why is honest, open communication so difficult sometimes? Your entry can be personal and not shared with the class.

While You Read

Reading Strategy Mini-Lesson

Reading Strategy ▶ Analyze Conflict and Resolution

As you recall from Chapter 3, the *conflict* is the major problem that a story's main character must overcome or solve. The *resolution* is the solution to the problem, or the outcome of the conflict. For example, think back to "Pluto," in Chapter 5. Rachel lands the lead in the senior play, but her parents are too preoccupied with her troublemaking sister to pay much attention to her. You could express the story's problem and resolution like this:

> *problem:* Rachel receives less attention from her parents than her older sister, a troublemaker, receives.

> *resolution:* Rachel realizes that she prefers being the family's "good" daughter rather than being the family troublemaker.

After identifying conflict and resolution, you can gain a deeper understanding of the story by **analyzing the conflict and resolution**. This reading strategy helps you see the relationship between minor conflicts in the story and the main conflict. It helps you make inferences about events in the plot and how they relate to the conflict and the resolution. You might think of this strategy as taking apart the conflict and resolution to see what makes them tick.

Asking questions like the ones in the following table will help you to analyze a story's conflict and resolution.

Analyzing Conflict and Resolution Questions to Ask	
Question	**Explanation**
1. What minor conflicts or problems help build the tension and contribute to the major conflict?	A minor conflict is one of the smaller problems in the plot. It helps build tension, it helps reveal the larger problem, and it forces the main character to move forward toward confronting the main problem. A character may solve several smaller problems before solving the main problem.
2. Does a specific event in the plot help reveal the conflict or the resolution?	Most events in a narrative reveal the main problem. Some events, however, foreshadow the resolution, reveal the resolution, or give hints about a cliff-hanger (unrevealed) resolution.
3. What kind of closure does the resolution give to the narrative?	The resolution can bring closure to a narrative in many ways. The main character may solve the problem, or he or she may accept that it never will be solved. The resolution may be thought provoking, sad, surprising, pleasing, or disturbing. Some resolutions are actually cliff-hangers—there are hints at how the main character will solve the problem, but the actual events are left to the reader's imagination.

Watch This!

The Strategy in Action

Refresh your memory of "Pluto" by scanning the story on pages 96–104. Then read the table on the next page. It shows how you might analyze conflict and resolution in this story.

Analyzing Conflict and Resolution in "Pluto"

Question	Example Responses
1. What minor conflicts or problems help build the tension and contribute to the major conflict? *Hint*: Resist the urge to simply list events here. List problems or conflicts, which are made up of one or more events.	Rachel faces several minor conflicts and problems before solving the main problem: —the problem of how to tell her family about the lead in the school play —the problem of feeling overlooked when Sara says she is converting to Episcopalianism —conflict at home when her parents and Sara disagree over Sara's decision —the problem of being overlooked in family therapy when the doctor does not ask her what she thinks —the problem of feeling unable to ask her parents to help her run lines or to talk about the play —challenges during rehearsals —internal conflict about whether to stay late at rehearsal without calling home
2a. Does a specific event in the plot help reveal the conflict?	These events help reveal the main conflict to me: —When Rachel announces that she got the lead in the play, Sara steals the show by announcing she is changing religions. —At family therapy sessions, the doctor is not interested in Rachel's point of view. —Rachel sits down to think about the consequences of not calling home to say she'll be late.

Question *continued*	Example Responses *continued*
2b. Does a specific event in the plot help reveal the resolution?	These events foreshadow or reveal the resolution: —Rachel sits down in the hallway to consider not phoning home and realizes that her parents won't even remember that she's in a play. Part of the resolution is that her mom does not remember, but Rachel decides to be okay with that. —Rachel looks in the mirror and wonders why she ever wanted to be the problem daughter. This hints that Rachel might realize that her role as the good daughter is okay after all. —The phone call home shows that Rachel has accepted her role as the good daughter.
3. What kind of closure does the resolution give to the narrative?	The resolution is a "feel-good" ending because Rachel feels good about herself and has come to terms with who she is within her family. No major questions are left unanswered, which gives solid closure.

Give It a Try

Analyze Conflict and Resolution

Directions: Refresh your memory of the first half of "Visit" by scanning the story on pages 240–243. We can express the main problem and resolution as follows:

> *Problem:* The father blames himself for his son's being in jail.
>
> *Resolution:* The father wants to ask the son for forgiveness.

Now read the second half of "Visit," beginning on page 251. As you read, complete the following table to analyze conflict and resolution in the remainder of the story. Read each question in the left column and write your responses in the right column.

**Analyzing Conflict and Resolution
in "Visit"**

Question	Response
1. What minor conflicts or problems help build the tension and contribute to the major conflict? *Hint*: Resist the urge to simply list events here. List problems or conflicts, which are made up of one or more events.	
2. Does a specific event in the plot help reveal the conflict or the resolution?	
3. What kind of closure does the resolution give to the narrative?	

Reading Selection

Visit

by Walter Dean Myers

continued from page 243

"I'm thinking about a new beginning, about starting my whole life all over again, and at the same time I know that this whole thing is going to end everything," he says. "Now I got this weight on me and I can't get out from under it."

Precious seconds pass before my mouth can open.

"I don't have all the answers," I say. "But sometimes I think that what we all have to do is to make peace within ourselves. To find our own connection with God and deal with that."

"When I got real scared," he says, "I was over at the market on 125th Street, you know where the train goes over and they sell candles and stuff underneath?"

"Yes."

"I was over there one morning," he says. "Real early. I couldn't sleep because I was so nervous after the story hit the papers. But I was thinking what you would feel if you saw my picture in the paper and everything."

"I was hurt," I lie.

Is the lie the better thing? Should I say I didn't know they were talking about a child of mine?

"I knew you would be, man," he says. He is asking for my pain to match his own. He starts to move his hand across the table, then stops and glances toward the guard in the corner of the room. We are not allowed to touch. "I knew you would be."

He turns his face away, and I know he is crying again. He is crying for himself, for this moment, and for all the moments that will never be.

The last time I saw him he was sullen, and he smelled of the cocoa butter his mother had smeared on his face to keep it from looking ashy. Her apartment was dirty; there were clothes piled in a corner. A straightening iron lay on the sink next to a bottle of cough medicine. They all had colds. Later, when it was time to leave, as I walked through the damp hallways I held my breath against the stench and made promises, to myself, of Christmas gifts that I would never fulfill.

Bless me, father, for I have sinned.

"And then what happened?" I ask.

"Then I got picked up and life just fell apart. The trial, lawyers, appeals, the whole nine yards," he says. "And here I am facing this heavy thing and I don't hear from nobody. But I know what's going down with you because she told me."

"She told you?"

"She told me that you and her met up and almost got married," he says. "She said her aunt didn't want her to marry you because you was too young or something."

I was nineteen and she was twenty-two, maybe twenty-three. She had long before acquired the habit of being used and I had the lust to use her.

"We were both so young," I say.

"So, what you been doing, man?"

"Not that much, really," I say.

> **Think critically about the conflicts as you read.**

Now it is time for my confession, but I can't bring myself to it. I struggle to just get through the minutes.

"You got hands like mine, long, skinny fingers like mine," he says.

"Yeah, your mom liked my hands," I say. "But we drifted apart, then we lost touch."

"She said she saw you in Brooklyn," he says.

"I was buying pastry at Junior's Restaurant," I said. "We met and had a few words. She was looking great."

She was looking terrible. Her skin, which had always been so smooth, had looked dull and dry. Her eyes, the bright, incredibly innocent eyes that had made me smile a thousand times, were distant and desperate.

I walked away from her, away from you.

"I've been doing well," I say.

"I'm glad to hear that," he says. "You know what I was thinking? I know it's impossible, but you know what I was thinking?"

"What?"

"I heard they write down your last day," he says. "What you do and what you eat and stuff."

I glance at the clock.

"The clock is a drag, huh?" he says.

"Yes, it is."

"What I been thinking about is, like when they write down the record and everything, they can write about you and me sitting here talking," he says. "Then when it's time to go, it's time to go. But, like, on the record, it's just me talking to my father. Like it's no big deal."

Bless me, father, for I have sinned.

"No big deal?" I push the words out.

"Somebody comes across the record—about what happened—and it's a regular . . . thing." A thin finger flicks away a drop of sweat on the still-unlined forehead. "You dig it?"

"I think I do."

"I'm real glad we got to sit down like this because it means a lot to me," he says. "Because I don't think I'm all that bad a person and I think you can get next to that. I'm just like an ordinary son. You know what I mean?"

"I don't know," I say. "I think I could have done better for you."

Precious seconds go by, and I think we both want to end them.

"No, you're okay," he says quickly. *He wants me to be okay.* "We both have to figure out some kind of thing to do. I got to go where I got to go, and you got to be moving on. But we're here talking and everybody's checking us out and putting it all down for the record so I guess it's cool."

So little. There will be a record of a father and son sitting and talking, having one last conversation, a babble of confessions tossed upon the fire.

"So I want to say . . . forgive me," I hear the words coming from my mouth. "So I want to say . . . forgive me and know that I know I haven't . . . haven't what?"

"Haven't done your best?" he says.

"Haven't done my best," I answer.

"We're embarrassed, right?" he says.

"I think so."

"You know, that's how I thought you would be," he says. "I thought we would be sitting here thinking the same things and feeling the same way."

"Damn, this is hard."

"Yo, don't cry man," he says. He touches my hand and the guard allows it. "It's not your fault. I threw it away. I just threw it all away. Sometimes it happens that way."

He pats my hand. He is comforting me. He smiles and stands before the guard gets to us. I had wondered if there would be a glass partition between us, or bars. There weren't. The last seconds in the visiting room are filled with his looking into my face and smiling. Him patting my hand in reassurance. Him saying good-bye.

There is one more scene. I sit with strangers, all of us uneasy in the grim theater of our fears. The curtains are closed. There is a nervous buzz of conversation in the room. I am tight with anticipation. In the corner of the room there is a nun, whiter than she is supposed to be, her habit darker than it should be. A million thoughts fly through my mind like demented harpies through the hot winds of hell. I look for the lofty thought, the God saving thought.

The curtains open. I know he will search for me. I know he has searched for me all of these years.

In the darkened theater there is a hush, a stillness that kills us all. His eyes find mine. They close.

Read-Aloud Opportunity ▶ Taking Parts

Directions: With your teacher's guidance, pair up with a classmate. Your teacher will assign the two of you a section of "Visit" to read aloud. One of you takes the part of the son and the other takes the part of the father. Read your section of the story aloud to the class. Just read the dialogue, not the narration.

After You Read

Converse

Directions: With your teacher's guidance, form groups of about five people. Begin a five-minute discussion of "Visit" by asking a question or making a comment about the story. If it's helpful, use one of the following prompts to phrase your question or comment. Listen as group members offer answers, opinions, and ideas in response to what you said. Repeat the process until each group member has initiated a five-minute discussion.

Question Prompts

Why did . . .

Why is this part in here . . .

What would happen if . . .

What does this part mean . . .

Do you think that . . .

Comment Prompts

This part is good because . . .

This part bothers me because . . .

I think that . . .

My favorite part is . . .

This part is confusing because . . .

Connect

Directions: Think of a time you and a parent or other adult had a hard time talking about something. Write a guide for adults with advice on how they should try communicating with teens. What should they realize about teenagers? What communication approach/style would be most effective? On your own paper, write a list of things that adults should know and understand when talking to children about any serious topic.

 **Write**

Directions: With your teacher's guidance, form small groups. Read aloud what each of you wrote in the Connect activity on the previous page. Share ideas and opinions about one another's advice and brainstorm for additional bits of wise counsel. Together, form a list of about ten items, called "Advice for Communicating with Those Close to You." Your teacher may ask your group to share your list with the class or post it on a wall.

Reflections

Parent-Child Relationships

This chapter opened with an illustration of a mother and daughter arguing. (See page 233.) Did you notice the close-ups from this illustration scattered throughout the chapter?

What did the main and smaller illustrations tell you about parent-child relationships? How does this relate to your own experience with a parent or guardian?

What ideas did the story give you about the topic?

Reread a Selection

Now that you've completed this volume, choose a strategy you learned (listed on page 271) that you think you need extra work on. Go back to your favorite selection from Chapters 6 through 11 and reread it on your own, using the strategy you chose. Then, on a separate piece of paper, answer the questions that follow.

1. **What selection did you pick?**

2. **What did you notice about the story the second time that you didn't notice the first?**

3. **How did that strategy make a difference in your reading?**

Read a New Selection

The following reading is an excerpt from the novel *Jazmin's Notebook* by Nikki Grimes. Read it and then answer the thought questions at the end.

from *Jazmin's Notebook*

by Nikki Grimes

APRIL 7

According to my sister, CeCe, the night before I was born, Mom and Dad sat in the living room, timing Mom's early contractions and arguing about my name during the minutes in between. They both agreed on the name itself, but spent half the night fighting about the spelling.

CeCe was six years old at the time, and would have been fast asleep, except that the tenement our family lived in on Lenox & 133rd was the size of a Cracker Jack box, with walls twice as thin, and sound carried easily from room to room. CeCe, in bed at the other end of the apartment, remembers laying wide-awake that night, listening to every word. She couldn't understand everything she heard, of course, but years later Mom filled in the details.

Apparently my father wanted my name to be a sort of homage to jazz. He sold life insurance for a living, but he was a frustrated sax man, and he figured if he couldn't spend his life playing jazz, he at least ought to be able to honor his love of "America's only original art form" by making it part of his baby daughter's name. He said this while Duke Ellington's "Sophisticated Lady" serenaded Mom from the stereo, mind you, so it's no wonder she got the hint. "Fine," she said. "We're well into the 50's, so why not *really* be modern and use a *y* in place of the *i*, while you're at it." But Dad said that was carrying things a bit too far. "Besides," he argued, "with a *y* instead of an *i*, people would be confused about the right way to pronounce the name." He won the argument, eventually, and so my birth certificate reads Jazmin Shelby. That's Jazmin with a *z*.

Now, that phrase might sound cute, but sometimes I find it downright annoying because I know I'll have to go through life repeating it over and over again. No one seems to get the spelling right on the first or second try.

I think it's great that Mom and Dad went to the trouble of making my name unique. But I've often considered changing it to Sally, or Linda, or maybe Jane, as in "See Jane run." That's one spelling everyone can manage. Of course, that kind of name wouldn't last me any longer than my straight perm did because I'm my own me, nappy hair and all, and truth is, Jazmin suits me best.

Folks will figure out how to spell my name sooner or later, I suppose, especially after they see it splashed across the jacket of my future best-seller (smile). Meanwhile, I've got my work cut out.

> 1. **Describe your experience reading the story excerpt. What strategies did you use from Chapters 6 through 11?**
>
> 2. **Would you want to read more of the novel? Explain.**

Appendix 1

About the Authors in This Volume

Nancy Werlin (1961–)

Nancy was born and raised near Salem, Massachusetts, which is uncanny since she writes psychological thrillers. She went to college at Yale, and then she moved to her current home near Boston. Nancy has a quirky writing habit: She checks the word count of her writing as she goes, kind of like a high school student writing a paper.

Kurt Vonnegut Jr. (1922–2007)

Kurt Vonnegut Jr. had many different jobs in his life: He was a soldier, he studied chemistry and anthropology, he worked for the General Electric Company, he was a writer. Vonnegut served in World War II and witnessed one of its most famous events: the fire bombing of Dresden, Germany. Vonnegut wrote mostly science fiction and satire. Some of his characters don't stay in their own stories but show up in his other stories as well.

Scott Westerfeld (1963–)

Scott is a summer chaser. He and his wife spend half the year in Sydney, Australia, and the other half in New York City, so it's always summer wherever they go. Scott is a vegetarian and a season ticket holder for the WNBA Liberty. His dad has done all kinds of interesting computer work, including on the Apollo space missions and on submarine projects.

David Klass (1960–)

David Klass preferred sports to reading when he was a kid. Actually, he still plays competitive soccer even though he's more of a reader now. Because of his early experience with books, David tries to write the kinds of books that might have interested him when he was younger. His first published piece of writing was a story called "Ringtoss," and it was published in *Seventeen* magazine while he was still in high school.

Megan Brady (1976–)

Megan wrote her first short story in fifth grade and won first place at her school's Language Arts Fair. She hasn't been able to stop writing since. Megan spent four years on the editorial staff of *Seventeen* magazine and currently works as a copywriter for Ralph Lauren. She has studied fiction with several teachers in New York City and belongs to the New York Writer's Workshop.

Gail Carson Levine (1957–)

Gail grew up in the Washington Heights neighborhood of New York City. She is the author of *Ella Enchanted*. Sound familiar? That's because it was made into a feature film in 2004. Gail likes to rework classic fairy tales like "Snow White" and "The Princess and the Pea" into her own full-length novels. She has a dog named Baxter, and she can bench-press more than half her own weight!

Sonya Sones

Sonya is multitalented and has done just about everything from hand painting dinosaurs and bunnies on baby clothes to working on films starring the actors Keanu Reeves and John Travolta. In fact, she worked as a consultant on the original movie version of *Grand Theft Auto*. Sonya's writing technique is to think of a question for her character right before she goes to sleep. In the morning, she takes a long walk and looks at everything through the eyes of her character. Then she writes it all down, not in regular writing (prose), but in verse (poetry).

Gloria Miklowitz (1927–)

Gloria's first writing job was as a scriptwriter for the Navy Department, where she wrote documentaries about rockets and torpedoes. These days she is writing young adult fiction and nonfiction about important issues like racial injustice, date violence, and steroid abuse. All of Gloria's children are published writers, and even her granddaughter is trying to become a writer.

Joan Bauer (1951–)

When Joan Bauer was growing up, she never quite felt like she fit. She always made jokes but found that her sense of humor was different from that of the people around her. Her parents' early divorce and a serious car accident taught her that adversity can make you stronger. Later in life, she became a writer with the goal of using humor to confront difficult issues.

Ralph Ellison (1914–1994)

Ralph Ellison's father believed in raising his son as a poet, and his mother was a social activist who was arrested many times for violating segregation laws.

Ellison received a full scholarship to Tuskegee University, but he dropped out and started writing. Much of Ellison's writing dealt with identity. His most famous book is *Invisible Man*, about a man who lives in New York, surrounded by millions of people, but who feels like nobody sees him. Ellison also studied music and was a talented trumpeter.

K. Ulrich (1968–)

K. Ulrich writes fiction and non-fiction. Her first book, *How to Write Your Life Story* was published in 2006 and she recently completed her first novel, *The Pourer Doesn't Always Stop on Time.* She lives and teaches in New York City and is inspired by whatever rides the cusp without cracking.

Angela Johnson (1961–)

Angela comes from a tight-knit family, and she tries in all her books to show the kind of love she experienced growing up. Before graduating college, Angela decided to become a writer. When she is writing, she says that she lives as though she is her characters, but if they come back to her to be revised before her book gets published, she gets annoyed with them, as though they are relatives who overstay their welcome.

Ben Mikaelsen (1952–)

Ben Mikaelsen is a true adventurer. He spent his early life in Bolivia and had all kinds of wild and wonderful pets. Right now, he lives in Montana with his pet black bear, Buffy. He has been to the North Pole, practiced the art of dog sledding, gone on a sixteen-hundred-mile cross-country horseback riding trip, and jumped out of airplanes. Ben has been writing since he was ten years old.

Walter Dean Myers (1937–)

Walter likes to tell the story of a time when he was reading a comic book and one of his teachers tore it up. She gave him some books, and he thinks that's the best thing that ever happened to him. Walter has a speech problem, and early on, he started to write as a more effective way to express himself. When he writes, Walter makes a collage of pictures of all his characters and hangs it over his desk. This way, he can look at them all the time while he's writing.

Appendix 2

Book Recommendations

If you liked . . .	Try . . .
The Rules of Survival by Nancy Werlin	• *Nobody's Family Is Going to Change* by Louise Fitzhugh • *How I Live Now* by Meg Rosoff • *Ironman* by Chris Crutcher
"Harrison Bergeron" by Kurt Vonnegut Jr.	• *Tangerine* by Edward Bloor • *Virtual War* by Gloria Skurzynski • *Feed* by M. T. Anderson • *Among the Hidden* by Margaret Peterson Haddix • *Truesight* by David Stahler Jr.
Uglies by Scott Westerfeld	• *So Much to Tell You* by John Marsden • *The Earth, My Butt, and Other Big Round Things* by Carolyn Mackler • *Perfect* by Natasha Friend • *The Plain Janes* by Cecil Castellucci
"Cradle Hold" by David Klass	• *Am I Blue?: Coming Out from the Silence*, edited by Marion Dane Bauer • *Getting the Girl* by Markus Zusak • *My Dad's Punk: 12 Stories About Boys and Their Fathers*, edited by Tony Bradman

If you liked . . . (*continued*)	Try . . . (*continued*)
"Last Dance" by Megan Brady	• *One Hot Second: Stories About Desire* (ed. Cathy Young) • *Behaving Bradley* by Perry Nodelman • *Nick & Norah's Infinite Playlist* by Rachel Cohn and David Levithan
"Pluto" by Gail Carson Levine	• *The Man in the Ceiling* by Jules Feiffer • *Kimani Tru: Pushing Pause* by Celeste O. Norfleet • *Gym Candy* by Carl Deuker
"Dr. Jekyll and Sister Hyde" by Sonya Sones	• *Make Lemonade* by Virginia Euwer Wolff • *The Geography of Girlhood* by Kirsten Smith • *It's Not Easy Being Mean* by Lisi Harrison • *The Wednesday Wars* by Gary D. Schmidt • *19 Varieties of Gazelle: Poems of the Middle East* by Naomi Shihab Nye
"Confession" by Gloria Miklowitz	• *Wrestling Sturbridge* by Rich Wallace • *The Outsiders* by S. E. Hinton • *Foxfire: Confessions of a Girl Gang* by Joyce Carol Oates

If you liked . . . (*continued*)	Try . . . (*continued*)
"A Letter from the Fringe" by Joan Bauer	• *Slot Machine* by Chris Lynch • *Geeks: How Two Lost Boys Rode the Internet Out of Ohio* by Jon Katz (nonfiction) • *The Chocolate War* by Robert Cormier • *The Perks of Being a Wallflower* by Stephen Chbosky
Invisible Man by Ralph Ellison	• *Dinky Hocker Shoots Smack!* by M. E. Kerr • *Dairy Queen* by Catherine Gilbert Murdock • *Jesse* by Gary Soto
"Kerri and Me" by K. Ulrich	• *The Truth About Forever* by Sarah Dessen • *A Certain Slant of Light* by Laura Whitcomb • *Olive's Ocean* by Kevin Henkes • *10 Things to Do Before I Die* by Daniel Ehrenhaft • *Pretty Little Liars* by Sara Shepard
"Through a Window" by Angela Johnson	• *Many Stones* by Carolyn Coman • *Fat Kid Rules the World* by K. L. Going • *Bullyville* by Francine Prose • *Stay With Me* by Garret Freymann-Weyr

If you liked . . . (*continued*)	Try . . . (*continued*)
Touching Spirit Bear by Ben Mikaelsen	• *Shark Bait* by Graham Salisbury • *Strays* by Ron Koertge • *Far North* by Will Hobbs
"Visit" by Walter Dean Myers	• *Bronx Masquerade* by Nikki Grimes • *Boot Camp* by Todd Strasser • *Angel's Grace* by Tracey Baptiste • *Looking for Alibrandi* by Melina Marchetta

Acknowledgments

Grateful acknowledgment is made to the following sources for having granted permission to reprint copyrighted materials. Every effort has been made to obtain permission to use previously published materials. Any errors or omissions are unintentional.

From THE RULES OF SURVIVAL by Nancy Werlin, copyright © 2006 by Nancy Werlin. Used by permission of Dial Books for Young Readers, A Division of Penguin Young Readers Group, A Member of Penguin Group (USA) Inc., 345 Hudson Street, New York, NY 10014. All rights reserved. Page 6.

"Harrison Bergeron" by Kurt Vonnegut, from WELCOME TO THE MONKEY HOUSE by Kurt Vonnegut Jr, copyright © 1961 by Kurt Vonnegut Jr. Used by permission of Dell Publishing, a division of Random House, Inc. Page 26.

From UGLIES by Scott Westerfeld. Reprinted with the permission of Simon Pulse, an imprint of Simon & Schuster Children's Publishing Division. Copyright © 2005 by Scott Westerfeld. Page 34.

"Cradle Hold" by David Klass, copyright © 1997 by David Klass, from NO EASY ANSWERS: SHORT STORIES ABOUT MAKING TOUGH CHOICES by Donald Gallo, editor. Used by permission of Random House Children's Books, a division of Random House, Inc. Page 51.

"Last Dance" by Megan Brady. Page 77.

Pluto Copyright © 2000 by Gail Carson Levine. First appeared in ON THE EDGE, published by Simon and Schuster Books for Young Readers. Reprinted by permission of Curtis Brown, Ltd. Page 96.

Excerpts from "Dr. Jekyll and Sister Hyde" by Sonya Sones, copyright © 2003 by Sonya Sones, from an anthology entitled NECESSARY NOISE, edited by Michael Cart. Reprinted by permission of Sonya Sones. Page 111.

"Confession" by Gloria D. Miklowitz, copyright © 1997 by Gloria D. Miklowitz, from NO EASY ANSWERS: SHORT STORIES ABOUT MAKING TOUGH CHOICES by Donald Gallo, editor. Used by permission of Random House Children's Books, a division of Random House, Inc. Page 127.

"A Letter from the Fringe" by Joan Bauer, copyright © 2001 by Joan Bauer, from ON THE FRINGE, edited by Donald R. Gallo. Used by permission of Dial Books for Young Readers, A Division of Penguin Young Readers Group, A Member of Penguin Group (USA) Inc., 345 Hudson Street, New York, NY 10014. All rights reserved. Page 151.

"Prologue," copyright 1952 by Ralph Ellison, from INVISIBLE MAN by Ralph Ellison. Used by permission of Random House, Inc. Page 177.

"Kerri and Me" by K. Ulrich. Page 192.

"Through a Window" by Angela Johnson, copyright © 2001 by Angela Johnson, from ON THE FRINGE, edited by Donald R. Gallo. Used by permission of Dial Books for Young Readers, A Division of Penguin Young Readers Group, A Member of Penguin Group (USA) Inc., 345 Hudson Street, New York, NY 10014. All rights reserved. Page 203.

From *Touching Spirit Bear* by Ben Mikaelsen. COPYRIGHT © 2001 by Ben Mikaelsen. Used by permission of HarperCollins Publishers. Page 217.

"Visit" by Walter Dean Myers. Reprinted by permission of Miriam Altschuler Literary Agency, on behalf of Walter Dean Myers. Copyright © 2003 by Walter Dean Myers. Page 240.

From JAZMIN'S NOTEBOOK by Nikki Grimes, copyright © 1998 by Nikki Grimes. Used by permission of Dial Books for Young Readers, A Division of Penguin Young Readers Group, A Member of Penguin Group (USA) Inc., 345 Hudson Street, New York, NY 10014. All rights reserved. Page 257.

Index

Strategy (*continued*)
understanding
foreshadowing and
flashback, 133–44
visualizing what the text
describes, 31–41
Suffixes, 125, 156–57
Summary, 81–87
key elements of, 83
length of, 85
writing, 87
Survey, reading habits, viii–ix

T
Tables, 2, 5, 74, 75, 76, 95, 106–7,
159, 199
IMO, 11, 234–35
word, 72
Taking parts, 254
Teacher-student shared-reading,
55, 69
Text
identifying genre of, 3, 4, 5
previewing, 3, 4, 5
questioning the, 22–30
visualization of, 31–41
Theme
defined, 179, 181
identifying, 179–86
variations in, 181
Thesaurus, 22, 159
Thought grid, 222, 225
"Through a Window" (Johnson),
203
Timelines, 126
Time order, words that signal,
125–26

Tone
defined, 199
identifying, 198–209
Touching Spirit Bear
(Mikaelsen), 217, 226

U
Uglies (Westerfeld), 34
Ulrich, K., 192, 261
Understanding
monitoring your, 11–20

V
Venn diagrams, 161–63, 167–68
"Visit" (Myers), 240, 251
Visualization
of text, 31–41
tips for, 34
Visuals
anticipation guide, 2, 20,
124, 188
boxes, 212
idea map, 180, 235–36
IMO Table, 11, 234–35
main idea bubble, 180
rating scales, 56–57, 207–8
tables, 2, 5, 95, 106–7, 146,
199
through grid, 222, 225
timelines, 126
Venn diagrams, 161–63,
167–68, 236
word association, 44–45
word grids, 22, 159–60
word table, 72
Vonnegut, Kurt, Jr., 26, 117,
259

W
Web page, creating, 105
Werlin, Nancy, 6, 16, 259
Westerfeld, Scott, 34, 259
Word association, 13, 44–45,
212
Word grids, 22, 159–60
tables, 159
Word parts, using, to determine
word's meaning, 156–57
Words
clue, 11, 147–49, 234–35
figurative meaning of, 172
finding meaning, in
context, 172–79
instant, 124–25
literal meaning of, 172
that signal comparison or
contrast, 161
that signal time order,
125–26
using word parts to
determine meaning of,
156–57
Word table, 72
Writing
advice column, 69–70
conversations, 197
figurative language in, 221
flashbacks, 143–44
free verse, 179
journal entries, 81
letters, 10
op-ed pieces, 132
pamphlets, 40, 209
poetry, 115
summary, 87

Strategies in This Book

Set a Purpose for Reading

Monitor Your Understanding

Question the Text

Visualize What the Text Describes

Identify Main Characters and Main Events

Identify Conflict and Resolution

Recall Story Details

Summarize a Story

Make Predictions

Make Connections

Identify Chronological Order

Understand Foreshadowing and Flashback

Recognize Cause and Effect

Make Comparisons and Contrasts

Find Word Meaning in Context

Identify Themes

Make Inferences and Draw Conclusions

Identify Tone and Mood

Interpret Figurative Language

Ask Questions to Discover Unstated Ideas

Compare and Contrast Unstated Ideas

Analyze Conflict and Resolution